Cooking Light® Quick & Easy Cookbook

Cooking Light®
QUICK & EASY COOKBOOK

COMPILED AND EDITED BY
SUSAN M. McINTOSH, M.S., R.D.

Oxmoor House®

Book Division of Southern Progress Corporation
P.O. Box 2465, Birmingham, Alabama 35201

Library of Congress Control Number: 00-136673
ISBN: 0-8487-2496-8
Printed in the United States of America
First Printing 2001

Previously published as *Low-Fat Ways to Cook Quick & Easy*
© 1995 by Oxmoor House, Inc.

Editor-in-Chief: Nancy Fitzpatrick Wyatt
Editorial Director, Special Interest Publications: Ann H. Harvey
Senior Foods Editor: Katherine M. Eakin
Senior Editor, Editorial Services: Olivia Kindig Wells
Art Director: James Boone

COOKING LIGHT® QUICK & EASY COOKBOOK

Menu and Recipe Consultant: Susan McEwen McIntosh, M.S., R.D.
Assistant Editor: Kelly Hooper Troiano
Foods Editor: Cathy A. Wesler, R.D.
Copy Editor: Shari K. Wimberly
Editorial Assistant: Julie A. Cole
Indexer: Mary Ann Laurens
Assistant Art Director: Cynthia R. Cooper
Designer: Carol Damsky
Senior Photographer: Jim Bathie
Photographers: Howard L. Puckett, Ralph Anderson
Senior Photo Stylist: Kay E. Clarke
Photo Stylists: Cindy Manning Barr, Virginia R. Cravens
Production and Distribution Director: Phillip Lee
Production Manager: Gail Morris
Associate Production and Distribution Manager: John Charles Gardner
Associate Production Manager: Theresa L. Beste
Production Assistant: Marianne Jordan

Cover: *Lemon Turkey Cutlets with Italian Asparagus (Recipes follow on page 27)*
Frontispiece: *Tropical Shrimp Salad (Recipe follows on page 93)*

We're Here for You!

We at Oxmoor House are dedicated to serving you with reliable information that expands your imagination and enriches your life. We welcome your comments and suggestions. Please write to us at:

Oxmoor House, Inc.
Editor, *Cooking Light®*
Quick & Easy Cookbook
2100 Lakeshore Drive
Birmingham, AL 35209

Contents

MAKE IT QUICK!

"I want to cut back on fat, but I just don't have the time!" Sound familiar? The mealtime answer for many busy families is a frozen dinner from the supermarket or a trip to the local burger factory—both of which can be sources of too much fat and sodium. "But diet recipes are so complicated!" you say. "Why can't low-fat cooking be easier?"

Now low-fat cooking can be easy with *Cooking Light Quick and Easy Cookbook*—a book designed for busy cooks who know that the key to a longer, healthier life is a low-fat diet that includes plenty of fiber.

Exercising and maintaining a healthy weight are also essential. And by spending less time in the kitchen, you will have more time to walk, jog, or take an aerobics class.

This collection of 200 kitchen-tested recipes has many features to help you cook with less fat in minutes instead of hours.

• **Quick recipes.** Each recipe takes less than 30 minutes of hands-on preparation, with no more than 45 minutes of total preparation time, including cooking. Menus can be prepared in under one hour. (Time for marinating or chilling is not considered part of the preparation time.)

• **Short ingredient lists.** While ingredient lists have been kept as short as possible, many recipes do call for common herbs, spices, and vegetable cooking spray. These lengthen the list of ingredients but add relatively little preparation time.

• **Low-fat convenience products.** These help keep cooking time and fat grams to a minimum.

• **Easy-to-read nutritional analyses.** Computed figures are provided at the end of every recipe.

• **Recommended accompaniments and cooking tips**. You will find suggestions for menu planning and recipe preparation throughout the book.

KITCHEN EQUIPMENT

The first step to quick, healthy meals is to organize your kitchen. A few basic tools will help you prepare low-fat recipes in less time.

• A **blender** can puree foods, make breadcrumbs, and blend beverages, sauces, and salad dressings. The blender's tall, narrow container makes it better than a food processor for processing small batches of food.

• A **colander** or **strainer** allows fat to drain from cooked ground meats and water to drain from pasta and other foods.

• **Two cutting boards** allow you to chop several ingredients for a recipe at one time; then use the ingredients as needed during cooking.

• An **egg separator** easily separates the low-fat egg white from the higher-fat yolk. It traps the thick yolk in the saucer and allows the white to slide through the slots.

• A **fat-off ladle** skims fat from the top of meat stocks, soups, and stews. When you pour liquids into a **gravy strainer**, the fat rises to the top, and the low-fat broth can be poured from a spout at the bottom of the cup.

• A **food processor** chops, slices, shreds, grinds, purees, and mixes food quickly and easily. A mini-chopper is good for mincing small quantities of fresh herbs or garlic.

• **Kitchen scissors** make easy work of trimming fat from meats and poultry, cutting fins off fish, cutting poultry into pieces, snipping fresh herbs, and cutting up some vegetables.

• **Knives** that are sharp will cut more quickly and cleanly than dull ones. Buy the best quality knives that you can afford because they will probably last a lifetime.

• A **loafpan** with drain holes is used mainly for meat loaf. The pan has a liner with holes that allow the fat from the meat loaf to drain into the outer pan away from the meat.

• Two sets of dry and liquid **measuring cups** and two sets of **measuring spoons** enable you to measure consecutive ingredients without washing or wiping out the measure repeatedly.

• An instant-read **meat thermometer** helps prevent overcooking and is especially helpful when cooking lean meats.

• **Nonstick skillets, saucepans, and baking pans** require less oil for cooking and are easy to clean.

• A **pizza cutter** can be used to cut dough and bread into small pieces.

• A **pressure cooker** can reduce cooking time by one-half to one-third for foods that require long moist-heat cooking, such as less tender, low-fat cuts of meat.

• **Scales** accurately measure ingredient amounts and portion sizes.

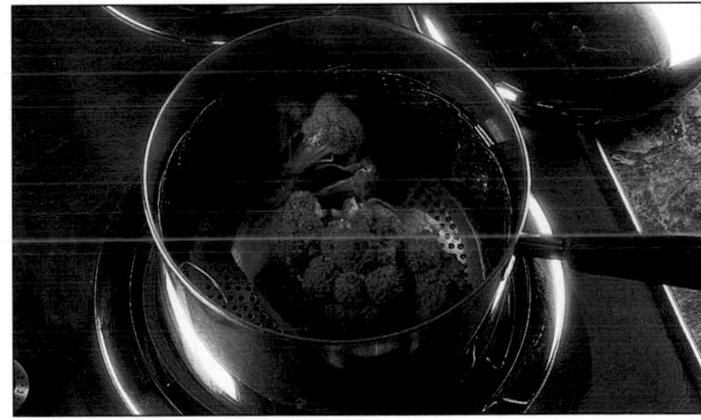

• A **steam basket or steamer** cooks vegetables, fruit, and fish with almost no fuss. You don't need to add fat to the steamed foods, and vitamin loss is minimal.

• A **vegetable peeler** peels vegetables and fruits quickly.

• A **wire grilling basket** prevents tender fish steaks, fillets, and vegetables from falling through the grill rack.

• A **wok** is useful for stir-frying, which is one of the quickest cooking methods; if the wok has a nonstick surface, you'll need to add little or no fat.

Menu Planning

The most successful, efficient cooks—those who can prepare meals that look and taste good with seemingly little effort—usually take time up front to get organized. That means planning menus, taking stock of the pantry and refrigerator, and making grocery lists before entering the supermarket. Here are some ways to increase your efficiency.

• Plan weekly menus to include your family's favorite recipes as well as new ones you want to try.

• Take an inventory of your pantry, refrigerator, and freezer, and then plan meals around what you have on hand, including leftovers. Fill in the "holes" with new recipes.

• Write out your grocery list as you plan menus so that you'll have all the ingredients on hand.

• Try to stick with the shopping list at the supermarket to shorten your trip and to avoid impulse buying.

• Always check a product's expiration date to be sure you're buying the freshest package.

• Keep a notepad and pencil in your kitchen to jot down ingredients that need replenishing.

Put Your Freezer To Work

• Label and date everything that goes into the freezer. Then rotate packages toward the front or the top of the freezer according to date.

• Keep a running inventory of the contents for efficient meal planning.

• Store food in small quantities. Cut up chicken, steaks, or chops and wrap each piece individually before storing in the freezer; then any number of pieces can be removed with ease when needed.

• Shape lean ground beef into patties or balls and wrap individually before freezing.

• Chop and freeze ½-cup quantities of onions, peppers, and parsley in zip-top freezer bags. Shred and freeze cheese in zip-top freezer bags.

• Keep the freezer at 0 degrees or colder, and you can keep prepared foods for up to two months, chicken and turkey parts for three months, and frozen fruits and vegetables for up to a year. Use a freezer thermometer to be sure of the temperature. Check periodically.

Safe Freezer Storage

Food	Storage time
Baked Goods	
Bread	3 months
Cakes	3 to 5 months
Cookies	6 months
Pies and pastry	2 months
Dairy	
Margarine	6 months
Cheese	4 months
Ice cream	1 to 3 months
Eggs: Whites	6 months
Yolks	8 months
Fish and Shellfish	
Fatty fish	3 months
Lean fish	6 months
Shellfish	3 months
Poultry	
Chicken, whole	3 to 6 months
Chicken, pieces	3 months
Chicken, cooked	1 month
Turkey	6 months
Meat	
Beef	6 to 12 months
Lamb	6 to 9 months
Pork	3 to 6 months
Veal	6 to 9 months
Ground meats	3 to 4 months
Ham	1 to 2 months
Bacon	1 month
Frankfurters	1 month
Variety meats	3 to 4 months
Leftover cooked meat	3 months
Vegetables and Fruits	
Vegetables, commercially frozen	8 months
Vegetables, home frozen	12 months
Fruits, commercially frozen	12 months
Fruits, home frozen	12 months

What To Buy

When shopping, look for convenience products that will help you cut minutes from preparation time and that are reduced-fat or nonfat versions of traditionally high-fat ingredients. Here are some of our favorites.

For the Pantry

Baking Supplies

Biscuit and baking mix, reduced-fat
Cake and cookie mixes, reduced-fat
Milk
- buttermilk powder
- canned evaporated skim milk
- instant nonfat dry milk powder

Muffin mix, reduced-fat
Pudding mix, instant
Roll mix, yeast
Vegetable cooking spray (butter-flavored, olive oil-flavored, or plain)

Fruits and Vegetables

Fruit
- canned, in light syrup or in juice
- dried
- juice, canned, unsweetened (100% juice)

Pasta sauce, low-fat, low-sodium
Red peppers in water, roasted
Tomatoes, sun-dried, dry-packed
Vegetables, canned, no-salt added

Grains, Legumes, and Pastas

Beans, canned, no-salt-added if available
Barley, quick-cooking
Bulgur, quick-cooking
Cereals, ready-to-eat high fiber, reduced- or low-fat
Couscous
Grits, quick-cooking or instant
Oats, quick-cooking or instant
Pasta, dry
Rice, boil-in-bag or instant
Rice and pasta mixes, reduced-fat, reduced-sodium

Condiments and Seasonings

(Some should be refrigerated after opening.)
Fruit spreads, low-sugar
Garlic, bottled minced fresh
Gingerroot, bottled minced fresh
Herbs and spices, dried
Jalapeño, bottled chopped
Mayonnaise, nonfat or reduced-fat
Salad dressing, oil-free or reduced-fat
Soy sauce, low-sodium
Worcestershire sauce, low-sodium

Miscellaneous

Bouillon granules (beef- and chicken-flavored)
Breadcrumbs, fine, dry
Broth, canned low-sodium (beef and chicken)
Soups, reduced-sodium, reduced-fat
Tuna, canned in water

For the Refrigerator

Cheese
- reduced-fat Cheddar and others
- nonfat or 1% low-fat cottage cheese
- nonfat or lite ricotta cheese
- nonfat or light process cream cheese product
- grated Parmesan cheese

Lemon juice, bottled fresh
Margarine, reduced-fat and regular
Milk, skim
Pasta, fresh
Sour cream, nonfat or reduced-fat
Yogurt, nonfat or low-fat
Vegetables, fresh, pre-prepared and bagged
- coleslaw mix
- mixed salad greens
- spinach

For the Freezer

Bagels and other breads
Chicken breast halves, skinned, boned
Egg substitute
Fruit juice concentrate, unsweetened
Fruit, unsweetened
Ice cream, nonfat
Meat and turkey, ground (frozen in 1-pound packages)
Sherbets and sorbets
Shrimp, cooked frozen
Vegetables, without added sauces or butter
Yogurt, frozen nonfat

Quick Tips

Make these tips part of your daily cooking routine to save cooking and cleaning time.

• Measure dry ingredients before moist ones to minimize cleanup.

• Rinse the measure with cold water before measuring honey and other sticky ingredients; the honey will slide out more easily.

• Chop an ingredient only once, even if it's called for in more than one step.

• Chop canned tomatoes right in the can with kitchen scissors.

• Get a head start on meal preparation by starting the night before. Almost any kind of food can be refrigerated overnight, and some recipes also freeze well. See the tips on page 8.

• Preheat the oven when baking or roasting to save time. It can reach the specified temperature while you are preparing the dish.

• Put foil in the bottom of a broiler pan and coat the broiler grid with vegetable cooking spray to prevent sticking.

• If you burn or scorch food in a pan, sprinkle the burned area liberally with baking soda, adding just enough water to moisten it. Let it stand for several hours before cleaning.

• Clean as you go. This saves time and makes the work easier.

• Rub a cut lemon on cutting boards and then wash the boards in soapy water to eliminate onion, garlic, or fish odors.

• Double recipes so that you make enough food for more than one meal—with only one shopping trip and one cleanup. Refrigerate or freeze the extra for another meal.

• Use your microwave oven to defrost foods. Set on defrost or use the MEDIUM-LOW (30% power) setting.

• Use your microwave oven to reheat foods. To save on cleanup, reheat and serve in the same dish.

Save Time—Microwave

An ideal low-fat cooking method, microwaving preserves flavor and nutrients without requiring fat. And because food cooks so quickly in a microwave, the flavors of many foods and herbs are actually enhanced. But before you put your microwave oven to work, be aware of the factors that affect cooking in it.

Wattage—Lower wattage ovens cook more slowly than those with higher wattage. The *Cooking Light Quick and Easy Cookbook* recipes are tested in 600- to 700-watt variable power ovens.

Size and shape of food—Irregularly shaped items cook differently than evenly shaped items. Small pieces cook faster than large, and sliced foods cook faster than whole.

Density—Dense, compact foods such as meat loaf will take longer to cook than porous foods such as muffins.

Quantity—As the quantity of food increases, so does the cooking time.

Moisture—Foods with a high moisture content, such as vegetables, fruits, fish, poultry, and sauces, are ideal for the microwave because moisture attracts microwave energy.

Fat and sugar levels—Foods with a high sugar or fat content heat more rapidly and tend to burn more easily than low-fat or unsweetened foods.

Temperature—Items taken directly from the freezer or refrigerator require a longer cooking time than those at room temperature.

Microwave Know-How

These techniques will help you achieve the best results when cooking, reheating, or defrosting in the microwave.

Arranging—Arrange foods such as chicken legs or broccoli spears with the thickest portion to the outside of the dish.

Covering—Use lids or heavy-duty plastic wrap to trap steam so that the food will cook faster and stay moist. Use wax paper to prevent splattering and paper towels to absorb moisture and fat.

Venting—Turn back one corner of the plastic wrap to prevent steam burns.

Piercing—Pierce foods with thick skins, such as potatoes, to allow steam to escape. (This will prevent bursting.)

Stirring—Stir foods while microwaving to promote even cooking.

Rotating—Rotate foods that cannot be stirred to ensure even cooking.

Standing time—Allow standing time for some foods so that they can finish cooking.

Converting Recipes

Some recipes convert well to the microwave just by shortening the cooking time; others need a few changes. For best results, follow these tips.

- Judge the best cooking temperature and time by looking at a microwave recipe that uses the same amounts of the main ingredients.
- Reduce liquid by about one-third because less liquid evaporates in microwave cooking.
- Shorten the cooking time to one-fourth or one-third the time suggested in the conventional recipe.
- Use slightly less seasoning because herbs tend to retain more flavor in the microwave.
- Follow the conventional recipe for dish size and covering, using a round dish when possible for even cooking. Also, keep in mind that mixtures that may boil and bubble, such as soups and sauces, require a deep dish.
- Some recipes that do not convert successfully to the microwave are meringues, popovers, and angel food cake. Rice and dried beans can be cooked in the microwave with good results, but you won't save much time over conventional methods.
- Sometimes only part of a recipe can be prepared in the microwave. For example, when you prepare pizza, make the sauce in the microwave but pop the pizza into the conventional oven to give it a crisp crust. You can't microwave yeast bread, but you can let it rise in the microwave if your oven has a LOW (10% power) setting.

Handy Substitutions

1 teaspoon baking powder	½ teaspoon cream of tartar plus ¼ teaspoon baking soda
1 cup beef or chicken broth	1 teaspoon beef- or chicken-flavored bouillon granules dissolved in 1 cup boiling water
1 cup nonfat buttermilk	¼ cup buttermilk powder plus water to equal 1 cup or 1 tablespoon vinegar or lemon juice plus skim milk to equal 1 cup
1 (1-ounce) square unsweetened chocolate	3 tablespoons unsweetened cocoa plus 1 tablespoon margarine
1 tablespoon cornstarch	2 tablespoons all-purpose flour
1 egg	¼ cup frozen egg substitute, thawed
1 cup sifted cake flour	1 cup sifted all-purpose flour minus 2 tablespoons
1 cup self-rising flour	1 cup all-purpose flour plus 1 teaspoon baking powder and ½ teaspoon salt
1 clove garlic	⅛ teaspoon garlic powder or ⅛ teaspoon minced dried garlic or ½ teaspoon bottled minced fresh garlic
1 tablespoon peeled, grated gingerroot	⅛ teaspoon ground ginger
1 tablespoon chopped fresh herbs	1 teaspoon dried herbs
½ cup honey	½ cup plus 2 tablespoons sugar plus 2 tablespoons water
1 tablespoon peeled, grated horseradish	2 tablespoons prepared horseradish
1 teaspoon grated lemon or orange rind	½ teaspoon lemon or orange extract
1 cup skim milk	½ cup evaporated skim milk plus ½ cup water or ¼ cup nonfat dry milk powder plus water to equal 1 cup
1 teaspoon dry mustard	1 tablespoon prepared mustard
1 cup tomato juice	½ cup tomato sauce plus ½ cup water
2 cups tomato sauce	¾ cup tomato paste plus 1 cup water
Wine	No-salt-added chicken or beef broth or unsweetened apple, orange, or white grape juice

Low-Fat Basics

Whether you are trying to lose or maintain weight, low-fat eating makes good sense. Research studies show that decreasing your fat intake reduces risks of heart disease, diabetes, and some types of cancer. The goal recommended by major health groups is an intake of 30 percent or less of total daily calories.

Cooking Light Quick and Easy Cookbook gives you practical, delicious recipes with realistic advice about low-fat cooking and eating. The recipes are lower in total fat than traditional recipes, and most provide less than 30 percent of calories from fat and less than 10 percent of calories from saturated fat.

If you have one high-fat item during a meal, you can balance it with low-fat choices for the rest of the day and still remain within the recommended percentage. For example, fat contributes 36 percent of the calories in Marinated Confetti Coleslaw for the Mississippi Fish "Fry" menu beginning on page 18. However, because the coleslaw is combined with other low-fat foods, the total menu provides only 25 percent of calories as fat.

The goal of fat reduction need not be to eliminate all fat from your diet. In fact, a small amount of fat is needed to transport fat-soluble vitamins and maintain other normal body functions.

Figuring the Fat

The easiest way to achieve a diet with 30 percent or fewer of total calories from fat is to establish a daily "fat budget" based on the total number of calories you need each day. To estimate your daily calorie requirements, multiply your current weight by 15. Remember that this is only a rough guide because calorie requirements vary according to age, body size, and level of activity. To gain or lose 1 pound a week, add or subtract 500 calories a day. (A diet of fewer than 1,200 calories a day is not recommended unless medically supervised.)

Once you determine your personal daily caloric requirement, it's easy to figure the number of fat grams you should consume each day. These should equal or be lower than the number of fat grams indicated on the Daily Fat Limits chart.

Daily Fat Limits

Calories Per Day	30 Percent of Calories	Grams of Fat
1,200	360	40
1,500	450	50
1,800	540	60
2,000	600	67
2,200	660	73
2,500	750	83
2,800	840	93

Nutritional Analysis

Each recipe in *Cooking Light Quick and Easy Cookbook* has been kitchen-tested by a staff of qualified home economists. Registered dietitians have determined the nutrient information, using a computer system that analyzes every ingredient. These efforts ensure the success of each recipe and will help you fit these recipes into your own meal planning.

The nutrient grid that follows each recipe provides calories per serving and the percentage of calories from fat. In addition, the grid lists the grams of total fat, saturated fat, protein, and carbohydrate, and the milligrams of cholesterol and sodium per serving. The nutrient values are as accurate as possible and are based on these assumptions.

- When the recipe calls for cooked pasta, rice, or noodles, we base the analysis on cooking without additional salt or fat.
- The calculations indicate that meat and poultry are trimmed of fat and skin before cooking.
- Only the amount of marinade absorbed by the food is calculated.
- Garnishes and other optional ingredients are not calculated.
- Some of the alcohol calories evaporate during heating, and only those remaining are counted.
- When a range is given for an ingredient (3 to 3½ cups, for instance), we calculate the lesser amount.
- Fruits and vegetables listed in the ingredients are not peeled unless specified.

SENSIBLE DINNERS

If panic sets in when the family asks, "What's for dinner?" then this chapter is for you. The six menus included feature a variety of ingredients but all have one thing in common—they're quick!

From a casual beef supper for the family to a festive crab dinner for company, you will be inspired by the many timesaving ideas and easy recipe combinations.

Feel free to mix and match the menu items based on what's in your pantry or refrigerator. In most cases we've suggested commercial bread, but if you'd like to make your own, turn to the Hurry-Up Breads chapter beginning on page 45 for ideas such as biscuits, muffins, corn sticks, or dressed-up Italian bread.

Sirloin with Sweet Red Pepper Relish, Garlic Potato Sticks, and Colorful Cabbage Salad *(menu on page 16)*

A Family Affair

(pictured on page 14)

This menu includes something for everyone—the kids will like the potato sticks, and you'll like the uncomplicated, quick recipes. Stir up the pudding first, and while it chills, make the relish and salad. Prepare and cook the potatoes, and then broil the steaks. Keep the menu easy with commercial dinner rolls (one per person).

Sirloin with Sweet Red Pepper Relish
Garlic Potato Sticks
Colorful Cabbage Salad
Commercial whole wheat dinner rolls
Banana Pudding Surprise
Iced tea

Serves 4
TOTAL CALORIES PER SERVING: 659
(CALORIES FROM FAT: 22%)

Sirloin with Sweet Red Pepper Relish

1 cup finely chopped sweet red pepper
½ cup finely chopped onion
¼ cup white wine vinegar
3 tablespoons sugar
⅛ teaspoon pepper
1 (1-pound) lean boneless beef sirloin steak
⅛ teaspoon salt
⅛ teaspoon pepper
Vegetable cooking spray

Combine first 5 ingredients in a saucepan. Bring to a boil; cover, reduce heat, and simmer 8 to 10 minutes or until tender. Remove from heat; keep warm.

Trim fat from meat. Cut meat into 4 equal pieces; sprinkle with salt and pepper. Place steaks on rack of a broiler pan coated with cooking spray. Broil 5½ inches from heat (with electric oven door partially opened) 6 to 8 minutes on each side or to desired degree of doneness.

To serve, transfer steaks to individual serving plates, and top evenly with red pepper mixture. Yield: 4 servings.

PER SERVING: 224 CALORIES (26% FROM FAT)
FAT 6.5G (SATURATED FAT 2.4G)
PROTEIN 26.4G CARBOHYDRATE 13.4G
CHOLESTEROL 76MG SODIUM 133MG

Family Fitness

People are more likely to maintain healthy physical fitness habits as adults if they develop them early in life. Encourage children to exercise at least 20 to 30 minutes each day with fun activities like running, skipping rope, in-line skating, and riding a bicycle.

Garlic Potato Sticks

2 medium baking potatoes (about 1 pound)
Vegetable cooking spray
2 teaspoons olive oil
2 cloves garlic, minced
1/8 teaspoon salt
1/8 teaspoon ground red pepper
1/8 teaspoon paprika

Cut potatoes into 2- x 1/4-inch strips. Place potato strips in a large bowl of ice water until slicing is complete. Drain potato; press between paper towels to remove excess moisture.

Coat a nonstick skillet with cooking spray; add oil. Place over medium heat until hot. Add potato strips, and cook 10 minutes. Add garlic, and cook an additional 10 to 15 minutes or until potato is lightly browned and tender, stirring frequently. Sprinkle with salt, pepper, and paprika. To serve, divide potato sticks evenly onto 4 individual serving plates. Serve warm. Yield: 4 servings.

Per Serving: 108 Calories (22% from Fat)
Fat 2.6g (Saturated Fat 0.3g)
Protein 2.6g Carbohydrate 19.4g
Cholesterol 0mg Sodium 82mg

Colorful Cabbage Salad

1 cup frozen mixed vegetables
1 cup preshredded cabbage with carrot
1/2 cup diagonally sliced celery
2 tablespoons commercial oil-free Italian dressing
1 tablespoon cider vinegar
1/8 teaspoon celery seeds
4 flowering kale leaves

Cook mixed vegetables according to package directions, omitting salt and fat. Drain and let cool. Combine mixed vegetables and next 5 ingredients. Cover and chill. To serve, place a kale leaf on each serving plate, and top each leaf with 1/2 cup vegetable mixture. Yield: 4 servings.

Per Serving: 39 Calories (30% from Fat)
Fat 0.3g (Saturated Fat 0.1g)
Protein 1.7g Carbohydrate 7.8g
Cholesterol 0mg Sodium 111mg

Banana Pudding Surprise

3 tablespoons sugar
2 tablespoons cornstarch
1/8 teaspoon salt
2 cups skim milk
2 egg yolks
1 cup sliced ripe banana (about 2 small)
3/4 teaspoon vanilla extract
2 tablespoons low-sugar strawberry spread
8 vanilla wafers, halved

Combine sugar, cornstarch, and salt in a heavy saucepan; stir well. Combine milk and egg yolks in a bowl; stir with a wire whisk. Gradually add to sugar mixture. Bring to a boil over medium-low heat, and cook 1 minute, stirring constantly. Remove from heat; stir in banana slices and vanilla.

Spoon 1/3 cup pudding into each of 4 dessert dishes; top each with 1 1/2 teaspoons strawberry spread and equal amounts of remaining pudding. Cover and chill. To serve, arrange 4 vanilla wafer halves around edge of each dish. Yield: 4 servings.

Per Serving: 212 Calories (20% from Fat)
Fat 4.8g (Saturated Fat 1.4g)
Protein 6.4g Carbohydrate 36.0g
Cholesterol 116mg Sodium 174mg

Oven-Fried Catfish, Baked Hush Puppies, and Marinated Confetti Coleslaw

Mississippi Fish "Fry"

Here, a favorite Southern supper gets a healthy twist. In fact, Oven-Fried Catfish and Baked Hush Puppies keep fat so low that each person can enjoy a whole catfish with three hush puppies, coleslaw, and two slices of tomatoes. Serve 1 cup watermelon per person to make dessert preparation easy.

Oven-Fried Catfish

Marinated Confetti Coleslaw

Sliced tomatoes

Baked Hush Puppies

Watermelon wedges

Iced tea

Serves 8

Total Calories per Serving: 420

(Calories from Fat: 25%)

Oven-Fried Catfish

6 (1-inch) slices French bread, cubed
1/4 cup nonfat mayonnaise
1 tablespoon plus 1 teaspoon water
8 (6-ounce) dressed catfish
Vegetable cooking spray
Lemon wedges (optional)
Fresh parsley sprigs (optional)

Position knife blade in food processor bowl; add bread cubes. Process 30 seconds or until breadcrumbs are fine. Sprinkle breadcrumbs onto an ungreased baking sheet; bake at 350° for 5 to 7 minutes or until lightly browned. Place breadcrumbs in a shallow bowl; set aside.

Combine mayonnaise and water; stir well. Dip fish in mayonnaise mixture; dredge in breadcrumbs. Place fish on a baking sheet coated with cooking spray. Bake at 450° for 15 to 17 minutes or until fish flakes easily when tested with a fork. To serve, transfer fish to individual serving plates. If desired, garnish with lemon wedges and fresh parsley sprigs. Yield: 8 servings.

Per Serving: 197 Calories (24% from Fat)
Fat 5.2g (Saturated Fat 1.2g)
Protein 22.0g Carbohydrate 13.3g
Cholesterol 65mg Sodium 298mg

Marinated Confetti Coleslaw

3 1/2 cups coarsely shredded cabbage
1 1/4 cups coarsely shredded red cabbage
1 cup coarsely shredded carrot
1 cup diced celery
1/2 cup chopped onion
3/4 cup cider vinegar
1/4 cup sugar
1 1/2 tablespoons vegetable oil
3/4 teaspoon dry mustard
1/2 teaspoon ground turmeric
1/2 teaspoon celery seeds
Small red cabbage leaves (optional)

Combine first 5 ingredients in a large bowl; toss mixture gently, and set aside.

Combine vinegar, sugar, oil, mustard, turmeric, and celery seeds in a small saucepan; bring to a boil over medium heat. Cook mixture until sugar dissolves, stirring occasionally. Pour over cabbage mixture; toss gently to coat. Cover and marinate in refrigerator at least 8 hours, stirring occasionally.

To serve, place a cabbage leaf on each individual serving plate, if desired. Toss coleslaw; using a slotted spoon, place 3/4 cup coleslaw onto each cabbage leaf. Yield: 8 servings.

Per Serving: 73 Calories (36% from Fat)
Fat 2.9g (Saturated Fat 0.5g)
Protein 0.9g Carbohydrate 12.5g
Cholesterol 0mg Sodium 26mg

Baked Hush Puppies

2/3 cup yellow cornmeal
1/3 cup all-purpose flour
1 teaspoon baking powder
1/2 teaspoon salt
1/8 teaspoon pepper
1/2 cup minced onion
1/3 cup skim milk
1/4 cup frozen egg substitute, thawed
1 tablespoon vegetable oil
Vegetable cooking spray

Combine first 6 ingredients in a medium bowl; make a well in center of mixture. Combine milk, egg substitute, and oil in a small bowl; stir well. Add to cornmeal mixture, stirring just until dry ingredients are moistened.

Spoon batter into miniature (1 3/4-inch) muffin pans coated with cooking spray, filling three-fourths full. Bake at 450° for 12 to 15 minutes or until hush puppies are lightly browned. Remove from pans immediately. Serve hush puppies warm. Yield: 2 dozen.

Per Hush Puppy: 31 Calories (26% from Fat)
Fat 0.9g (Saturated Fat 0.2g)
Protein 0.9g Carbohydrate 4.8g
Cholesterol 0mg Sodium 67mg

Pork Stir-Fry with Tri-Color Peppers and Parslied Rice

Dinner on the Double

Need a healthy meal for the family? You can have this nutritious dinner ready in just under 45 minutes. While the rice is cooking, slice the vegetables and prepare the stir-fry. It will be completed by the time the rice is done. Commercial hard rolls (one per serving) and a super-easy fruit dessert accompany the meal.

Pork Stir-Fry with Tri-Color Peppers
Parslied Rice
Commercial hard rolls
Amaretti-Topped Fruit
Sparkling water

Serves 4
Total Calories per Serving: 488
(Calories from Fat: 15%)

Pork Stir-Fry with Tri-Color Peppers

1 pound pork tenderloin
1 teaspoon dark sesame oil
1 tablespoon low-sodium soy sauce
¼ teaspoon garlic powder
¼ teaspoon ground ginger
¼ teaspoon ground cumin
1 cup slivered onion
¾ cup julienne-sliced green pepper
¾ cup julienne-sliced sweet red pepper
¾ cup julienne-sliced sweet yellow pepper
2 tablespoons white wine vinegar

Trim fat from pork, and cut pork crosswise into ¼-inch slices. Heat oil in a large nonstick skillet over high heat until hot. Add pork, soy sauce, and next 3 ingredients to skillet; stir-fry 3 minutes or until pork is done. Remove mixture from skillet; set aside, and keep warm.

Place skillet over medium-high heat; add onion and peppers, and stir-fry 5 minutes. Return pork mixture to skillet; add vinegar, and cook 1 minute. Yield: 4 (1-cup) servings.

Per Serving: 171 Calories (23% from Fat)
Fat 4.3g (Saturated Fat 1.2g)
Protein 24.8g Carbohydrate 6.9g
Cholesterol 74mg Sodium 157mg

Parslied Rice

1 cup water
⅛ teaspoon salt
½ cup long-grain rice, uncooked
2 tablespoons chopped fresh parsley
1 teaspoon margarine

Bring water and salt to a boil in a saucepan; add rice. Cover, reduce heat, and simmer 20 minutes or until liquid is absorbed. Stir in parsley and margarine. Yield: 4 (½-cup) servings.

Per Serving: 94 Calories (11% from Fat)
Fat 1.1g (Saturated Fat 0.2g)
Protein 1.7g Carbohydrate 18.6g
Cholesterol 0mg Sodium 87mg

Amaretti-Topped Fruit

1½ cups sliced banana (about 2 medium)
1 (15¾-ounce) can unsweetened pineapple chunks, undrained
4 (1½-inch) amaretti cookies, crushed

Combine banana and pineapple; toss gently. To serve, spoon into 4 dessert dishes; top with cookie crumbs. Yield: 4 servings.

Per Serving: 140 Calories (7% from Fat)
Fat 1.1g (Saturated Fat 0.3g)
Protein 0.8g Carbohydrate 32.8g
Cholesterol 3mg Sodium 18mg

SUPPER ON THE BAYOU

Make the Vanilla Pudding ahead of time, and this Cajun-inspired meal can be prepared and served in less than one hour. To dress up the commercial French bread, cut it into ½-inch-thick slices. Coat each slice with butter-flavored vegetable cooking spray, and broil until crisp and lightly browned. (The analysis includes two slices of bread per serving.)

Cajun-Spiced Chicken
Spicy Bow Ties
Commercial French bread
Vanilla Pudding

Serves 4
TOTAL CALORIES PER SERVING: 608
(CALORIES FROM FAT: 14%)

Cajun-Spiced Chicken and Spicy Bow Ties

Cajun-Spiced Chicken

½ teaspoon dried Italian seasoning
½ teaspoon paprika
½ teaspoon ground red pepper
¼ teaspoon onion powder
¼ teaspoon garlic powder
¼ teaspoon ground white pepper
¼ teaspoon freshly ground black pepper
4 (4-ounce) skinned, boned chicken breast halves
2 teaspoons olive oil

Combine first 7 ingredients in a heavy-duty, zip-top plastic bag. Place one chicken breast half in bag; seal bag, and shake until chicken is coated. Remove chicken, and repeat procedure with remaining chicken.

Heat olive oil in a large nonstick skillet over medium heat until hot. Add chicken, and cook 3 to 4 minutes on each side or until chicken is lightly browned and done. Yield: 4 servings.

Per Serving: 149 Calories (23% from Fat)
Fat 3.8g (Saturated Fat 0.7g)
Protein 26.4g Carbohydrate 0.9g
Cholesterol 66mg Sodium 74mg

Spicy Bow Ties

Vegetable cooking spray
1 teaspoon vegetable oil
1 small sweet red pepper, seeded and chopped
½ cup frozen English peas, thawed
2 green onions, cut into 1-inch pieces
⅔ cup nonfat sour cream
2 tablespoons skim milk
⅛ to ¼ teaspoon ground red pepper
⅛ teaspoon chili powder
2 to 4 drops of hot sauce
1 clove garlic, crushed
4 ounces farfalle (bow tie pasta), uncooked

Coat a large nonstick skillet with cooking spray; add oil. Place over medium-high heat until hot. Add sweet red pepper and peas; sauté 2 to 3 minutes or until vegetables are crisp-tender. Add green onions, and sauté 30 seconds or until onions are barely limp. Remove from heat, and keep warm.

Combine sour cream and next 5 ingredients in a small bowl; stir well. Set aside.

Cook pasta according to package directions, omitting salt and fat; drain. Place in a serving bowl. Add vegetable mixture and sour cream mixture; toss. Serve immediately. Yield: 4 (¾-cup) servings.

Per Serving: 176 Calories (10% from Fat)
Fat 2.0g (Saturated Fat 0.2g)
Protein 8.1g Carbohydrate 28.9g
Cholesterol 0mg Sodium 62mg

Vanilla Pudding

½ cup sugar
2½ tablespoons cornstarch
⅛ teaspoon salt
2 cups skim milk
1 egg, lightly beaten
1 tablespoon reduced-calorie margarine
2 teaspoons vanilla extract

Combine first 3 ingredients in a heavy saucepan. Combine milk and egg; stir well. Add to dry ingredients. Cook over medium heat, stirring constantly, until pudding mixture comes to a boil.

Remove pudding mixture from heat; stir in margarine and vanilla. Pour mixture into 4 (6-ounce) custard cups. Cover with plastic wrap, gently pressing directly onto pudding. Chill at least 45 minutes. Yield: 4 (½-cup) servings.

Per Serving: 201 Calories (15% from Fat)
Fat 3.3g (Saturated Fat 0.8g)
Protein 5.8g Carbohydrate 36.4g
Cholesterol 58mg Sodium 182mg

Menu Helper

If you didn't make Vanilla Pudding in time, try Orange Parfaits on page 133.

Elegant Seafood Dinner

Your guests won't believe you spent so little time in the kitchen when you present this beautiful dinner. Get a head start by preparing the rice salad, dessert sauce, and fruit earlier in the day. Just before serving, steam the vegetables. While these cook, assemble the crab mixture. Two minutes before serving, broil the Crab Mornay. Complement the dinner with commercial rolls (one per person) and white wine (6 ounces per person). Spoon the chilled sauce over the fruit just before serving.

Crab Mornay

Tarragon Carrots and Broccoli

Curried Rice Salad

Commercial hard rolls

Fresh Fruit with Cointreau Sauce

White wine

Serves 4
TOTAL CALORIES PER SERVING: 645
(CALORIES FROM FAT: 14%)

Crab Mornay

½ cup Chablis or other dry white wine
¼ cup water
1 teaspoon chicken-flavored bouillon granules
Dash of ground white pepper
1 cup sliced fresh mushrooms
2 tablespoons sliced green onions
¼ cup skim milk
1 tablespoon cornstarch
½ cup (2 ounces) shredded reduced-fat Jarlsberg or Swiss cheese
⅔ pound lump crabmeat
1 (2-ounce) jar chopped pimiento, drained
Green onion fans (optional)

Combine first 4 ingredients in a small saucepan; bring to a boil. Add mushrooms and sliced onions. Cover, reduce heat, and simmer 1 minute or until mushrooms are tender.

Combine milk and cornstarch; add to mushroom mixture. Bring to a boil over medium heat; boil 1 minute, stirring constantly. Remove from heat; add cheese, and stir until melted. Stir in crabmeat and pimiento. Spoon into 4 (6-ounce) ramekins or custard cups. Broil 2 minutes or until bubbly. Garnish with onion fans, if desired. Yield: 4 servings.

PER SERVING: 149 CALORIES (22% FROM FAT)
FAT 3.6G (SATURATED FAT 1.6G)
PROTEIN 21.7G CARBOHYDRATE 5.7G
CHOLESTEROL 76MG SODIUM 566MG

Menu Helper

To make the green onion fans shown on page 25, cut off the white portion of the onion. Slice the green portion into thin strips from both ends, cutting almost to but not through the center. Place in ice water, and chill until strips curl.

Crab Mornay, Curried Rice Salad, and Tarragon Carrots and Broccoli

Tarragon Carrots and Broccoli

2 cups fresh broccoli flowerets
2 cups diagonally sliced carrot
1½ teaspoons reduced-calorie margarine
1 teaspoon dried tarragon

Arrange broccoli flowerets and carrot in a vegetable steamer over boiling water; cover and steam 8 minutes or until crisp-tender. Transfer to a serving bowl. Add margarine, and sprinkle with tarragon. Toss lightly until margarine melts. Yield: 4 (¾-cup) servings.

Per Serving: 46 Calories (23% from Fat)
Fat 1.2g (Saturated Fat 0.2g)
Protein 1.8g Carbohydrate 8.4g
Cholesterol 0mg Sodium 45mg

Curried Rice Salad

1 cup cooked long-grain rice (cooked without salt or fat)
½ cup chopped celery
¼ cup minced fresh chives
¼ cup chopped sweet red pepper
¼ cup commercial reduced-calorie Italian dressing
2 teaspoons vinegar
1 teaspoon curry powder
2 tablespoons slivered almonds, toasted
4 Bibb lettuce leaves (optional)

Combine first 4 ingredients. Combine dressing, vinegar, and curry powder; add to rice mixture, and toss well. Cover and chill.

To serve, stir in almonds, and spoon mixture over lettuce leaves, if desired. Yield: 4 servings.

Per Serving: 100 Calories (28% from Fat)
Fat 3.1g (Saturated Fat 0.3g)
Protein 2.7g Carbohydrate 16.1g
Cholesterol 0mg Sodium 179mg

Fresh Fruit with Cointreau Sauce

If you prefer, combine the yogurt with orange juice instead of Cointreau.

½ cup vanilla low-fat yogurt
2½ tablespoons Cointreau or other orange-flavored liqueur
4 medium oranges, peeled, sectioned, and seeded
1 cup seedless green grapes
1 cup sliced fresh strawberries
Fresh mint sprigs (optional)

Combine yogurt and liqueur in a small bowl; cover and chill.

Layer fruit evenly in individual dessert dishes; cover and chill. To serve, spoon chilled yogurt sauce evenly over fruit. Garnish with mint, if desired. Yield: 4 servings.

Per Serving: 155 Calories (5% from Fat)
Fat 0.9g (Saturated Fat 0.4g)
Protein 3.1g Carbohydrate 31.8g
Cholesterol 1mg Sodium 20mg

Quick Tip

Really pushed for time? Washing and slicing vegetables and fruit can take time you may not have to spare. If so, look to your supermarket salad bar for items on your grocery list. You may be able to purchase the mushrooms, green onions, broccoli, celery, red pepper, and fruit already washed and cut for your entrée, side dish, salad, and dessert.

After-Work Entertaining

(pictured on cover)

With the ingredients for this menu in your refrigerator, you can serve a lovely dinner only an hour after arriving home. (Allow one roll and one scoop of ice cream per person.)

Lemon Turkey Cutlets
Italian Asparagus
Commercial sourdough rolls
Ice Cream with Dark Chocolate Sauce

Serves 4
TOTAL CALORIES PER SERVING: 487
(CALORIES FROM FAT: 13%)

Lemon Turkey Cutlets

8 (2-ounce) turkey breast cutlets
2½ tablespoons all-purpose flour
2 teaspoons olive oil, divided
¼ teaspoon salt
¼ teaspoon freshly ground pepper
2 tablespoons lemon juice
1 lemon, sliced (optional)
Fresh sage sprigs (optional)

Place cutlets between 2 sheets of heavy-duty plastic wrap; flatten to ⅛-inch thickness, using a meat mallet or rolling pin. Dredge in flour; set aside.

Heat 1 teaspoon oil in a large nonstick skillet over medium heat until hot. Add half of cutlets, and cook 3 minutes on each side or until browned. Transfer cutlets to a serving platter; keep warm. Repeat procedure with remaining 1 teaspoon oil and cutlets. Sprinkle cutlets with salt, pepper, and lemon juice. If desired, garnish with lemon slices and fresh sage sprigs. Yield: 4 servings.

PER SERVING: 179 CALORIES (26% FROM FAT)
FAT 5.2G (SATURATED FAT 1.2G)
PROTEIN 26.8G CARBOHYDRATE 4.5G
CHOLESTEROL 61MG SODIUM 203MG

Italian Asparagus

1 pound fresh asparagus spears
¾ cup chopped tomato
2 tablespoons chopped green onions
⅛ teaspoon dried oregano
⅛ teaspoon dried thyme
⅛ teaspoon pepper
2 teaspoons freshly grated Parmesan cheese

Snap off tough ends of asparagus. Remove scales from stalks with a knife or vegetable peeler, if desired. Arrange asparagus in a vegetable steamer over boiling water. Cover and steam 4 to 5 minutes or until crisp-tender; keep warm.

Combine tomato and next 4 ingredients in a small bowl; stir well. To serve, spoon tomato mixture over asparagus; sprinkle with cheese. Yield: 4 servings.

PER SERVING: 28 CALORIES (19% FROM FAT)
FAT 0.6G (SATURATED FAT 0.2G)
PROTEIN 2.8G CARBOHYDRATE 4.6G
CHOLESTEROL 1MG SODIUM 24MG

Ice Cream with Dark Chocolate Sauce

2 tablespoons plus 2 teaspoons unsweetened cocoa
1½ tablespoons sifted powdered sugar
1½ teaspoons cornstarch
⅓ cup light-colored corn syrup
2 tablespoons plus 2 teaspoons water
½ teaspoon vanilla extract
2 cups nonfat vanilla ice cream

Combine first 3 ingredients in a small saucepan. Gradually stir in corn syrup and water. Cook over medium heat, stirring constantly, until thickened. Remove from heat; stir in vanilla. Serve warm or chilled over ½ cup ice cream. Yield: 4 servings.

PER SERVING: 211 CALORIES (2% FROM FAT)
FAT 0.5G (SATURATED FAT 0.3G)
PROTEIN 3.0G CARBOHYDRATE 47.3G
CHOLESTEROL 0MG SODIUM 75MG

SIMPLE BEGINNINGS

A carton of dip and a bag of chips may be your idea of a quick appetizer. Or, if you're health-conscious, you may prefer carrot sticks and cottage cheese. But with the recipes in this chapter, you'll find that you can have much better choices than these—even if you're pressed for time.

If you have fresh fruit on hand, try Fruit Kabobs (page 30) with a simple yogurt dip. Another time, make your own low-fat tortilla or bagel chips, or try our version of an ever-popular snack mix (page 36).

And don't forget beverages. We've included several recipes for both hot and cold drinks. Serve these thirst-quenchers with appetizers or by themselves as a snack—they are good anytime.

Mock Margaritas (recipe on page 39) and Garbanzo Guacamole (recipe on page 33)

Salsa with Pita Chips

1¼ cups chopped tomato
2½ tablespoons chopped green onions
2 tablespoons cold water
1½ teaspoons chopped fresh cilantro
1½ teaspoons fresh lime juice
½ teaspoon minced jalapeño pepper
¼ teaspoon salt
3 (8-inch) pita bread rounds

Combine first 7 ingredients in a medium bowl; stir well. Cover and chill salsa at least 1 hour.

Separate each pita bread round; cut each round into 4 wedges, and place on an ungreased baking sheet. Bake at 400° for 7 minutes or until lightly browned. Arrange 4 chips around ¼ cup salsa for each serving. Yield: 6 appetizer servings.

Per Serving: 100 Calories (7% from Fat)
Fat 0.8g (Saturated Fat 0.9g)
Protein 2.2g Carbohydrate 19.5g
Cholesterol 0mg Sodium 194mg

Fruit Kabobs

You may omit the rum and thus the marinating time, if you'd prefer.

32 fresh pineapple chunks (about 1 pound)
32 small strawberries (about 3 cups)
32 honeydew melon balls (about 3 cups)
¼ cup rum
8 ounces reduced-fat Havarti or Monterey Jack cheese, cut into 32 cubes
2 (8-ounce) cartons strawberry low-fat yogurt
½ teaspoon ground cardamom

Combine first 4 ingredients; toss gently to coat. Cover and chill 4 hours, stirring occasionally.

Thread fruit and cheese onto 32 (6-inch) wooden skewers. Combine yogurt and cardamom; stir well. Serve kabobs with dip. Yield: 32 appetizers.

Per Appetizer: 56 Calories (26% from Fat)
Fat 1.6g (Saturated Fat 0.9g)
Protein 2.8g Carbohydrate 7.4g
Cholesterol 5mg Sodium 55mg

Orange-Poppy Seed Dip

½ cup vanilla low-fat yogurt
¼ cup light process cream cheese product, softened
¼ cup orange marmalade
1 teaspoon poppy seeds
Orange rind curls (optional)

Spoon yogurt onto several layers of heavy-duty paper towels, and spread to ½-inch thickness. Cover with additional paper towels; let stand 5 minutes. Scrape yogurt into a medium bowl.

Add cream cheese to yogurt. Beat at medium speed of an electric mixer until smooth. Stir in marmalade and poppy seeds. Cover and chill.

Stir before serving. Garnish with orange curls, if desired. Serve with fresh fruit. Yield: ¾ cup.

Per Tablespoon: 36 Calories (25% from Fat)
Fat 1.0g (Saturated Fat 0.6g)
Protein 1.0g Carbohydrate 6.1g
Cholesterol 3mg Sodium 36mg

Piña Colada Dip

2 (8-ounce) cartons pineapple low-fat yogurt
¼ cup finely chopped dried apricots
1 tablespoon minced crystallized ginger
1 teaspoon coconut extract
½ teaspoon rum extract

Place a colander in a 2-quart glass measure. Line colander with 4 layers of cheesecloth; allow cheesecloth to extend over edges of colander.

Stir yogurt until smooth. Spoon yogurt into colander, and cover yogurt loosely with plastic wrap; chill 12 hours. Spoon yogurt cheese into a medium bowl; discard liquid.

Add apricots and remaining ingredients to yogurt; stir well. Serve with fresh fruit. Yield: 1¼ cups.

Per Tablespoon: 29 Calories (9% from Fat)
Fat 0.3g (Saturated Fat 0.2g)
Protein 1.0g Carbohydrate 5.6g
Cholesterol 1mg Sodium 13mg

Orange-Poppy Seed Dip

Dilly Clam Dip

Dilly Clam Dip

1 (6½-ounce) can minced clams, undrained
½ teaspoon dried dillweed
¾ cup 1% low-fat cottage cheese
2 tablespoons light process cream cheese product
1 tablespoon finely chopped onion
2 teaspoons lemon juice
6 drops of hot sauce

Drain clams, reserving 3 tablespoons liquid; set aside. Place reserved clam liquid, dillweed, and remaining ingredients in container of an electric blender or food processor; cover and process until smooth. Spoon mixture into a bowl; stir in clams. Serve with raw vegetables. Yield: 1½ cups.

PER TABLESPOON: 12 CALORIES (23% FROM FAT)
FAT 0.3G (SATURATED FAT 0.2G)
PROTEIN 1.6G CARBOHYDRATE 0.6G
CHOLESTEROL 3MG SODIUM 80MG

Garbanzo Guacamole

(pictured on page 28)

⅔ cup canned garbanzo beans, drained
1 tablespoon lemon juice
1 large clove garlic, halved
¾ cup coarsely chopped onion
½ cup peeled, cubed avocado
2 tablespoons canned chopped green chiles
¼ teaspoon salt
¼ teaspoon pepper
1 cup seeded, finely chopped tomato
½ cup finely chopped green onions
12 (6-inch) corn tortillas
Cherry tomatoes (optional)

Position knife blade in food processor bowl; add beans, lemon juice, and garlic. Process 20 seconds, scraping sides of processor bowl once. Add onion and next 4 ingredients; pulse 5 times or until mixture is chunky.

Transfer mixture to a medium bowl; stir in tomato and green onions. Cover; chill thoroughly.

Cut each tortilla into 6 wedges; arrange on a large ungreased baking sheet. Bake at 350° for 6 to 8 minutes or until crisp. Serve guacamole with tortilla wedges. Garnish with cherry tomatoes, if desired. Yield: 3 dozen appetizer servings.

PER SERVING: 33 CALORIES (22% FROM FAT)
FAT 0.8G (SATURATED FAT 0.1G)
PROTEIN 1.1G CARBOHYDRATE 5.8G
CHOLESTEROL 0MG SODIUM 35MG

Salmon Canapés

¼ cup finely chopped green onions
¼ teaspoon dried dillweed
⅛ teaspoon ground white pepper
¼ cup nonfat process cream cheese product, softened
1 teaspoon skim milk
16 slices party-style pumpernickel bread, toasted
1 (4-ounce) package thinly sliced smoked salmon
Fresh dill sprigs (optional)

Combine first 5 ingredients in a small bowl; stir well. Spread 1 teaspoon cream cheese mixture over each bread slice; top with salmon. Garnish with dill sprigs, if desired. Yield: 16 appetizers.

PER APPETIZER: 28 CALORIES (13% FROM FAT)
FAT 0.4G (SATURATED FAT 0.1G)
PROTEIN 2.5G CARBOHYDRATE 3.7G
CHOLESTEROL 2MG SODIUM 115MG

Fat Alert

Whip up your own tortilla or pita chips and cut the fat. One ounce of commercial tortilla chips contains 8.0 grams of fat and 140 calories, while the same amount of homemade tortilla chips in the Garbanzo Guacamole recipe has only 0.9 gram of fat and 76 calories.

Hot Artichoke and Parmesan Spread

1 cup 1% low-fat cottage cheese
½ cup grated Parmesan cheese
2 tablespoons nonfat mayonnaise
2 tablespoons plain nonfat yogurt
1 clove garlic, minced
⅛ teaspoon hot sauce
1 (14-ounce) can artichoke hearts, drained and finely chopped
Vegetable cooking spray
48 whole wheat Melba rounds

Position knife blade in food processor bowl; add first 6 ingredients. Process until smooth, scraping sides of processor bowl once. Transfer mixture to a bowl; stir in artichokes.

Spoon artichoke mixture into a 1-quart baking dish coated with cooking spray. Bake at 350° for 20 minutes or until thoroughly heated. Serve with Melba rounds. Yield: 16 appetizer servings.

Per Serving: 73 Calories (17% from Fat)
Fat 1.4g (Saturated Fat 0.8g)
Protein 4.7g Carbohydrate 10.3g
Cholesterol 3mg Sodium 158mg

Cheese Tortellini with Basil Sauce

½ (9-ounce) package fresh cheese tortellini, uncooked
1 (8-ounce) can no-salt-added tomato sauce
1 clove garlic, crushed
½ teaspoon dried basil
¼ teaspoon dried oregano
1 tablespoon grated Parmesan cheese

Cook tortellini according to package directions, omitting salt and fat. Drain; keep warm.

Combine tomato sauce, crushed garlic, basil, and oregano in a small saucepan; bring to a boil. Cover, reduce heat, and simmer 5 minutes; slowly stir in Parmesan cheese.

To serve, transfer basil sauce to a serving bowl. Serve tortellini with warm sauce. Yield: 14 appetizer servings.

Per Serving: 36 Calories (23% from Fat)
Fat 0.9g (Saturated Fat 0.3g)
Protein 1.8g Carbohydrate 7.2g
Cholesterol 6mg Sodium 45mg

Miniature Chicken Tostadas

Jicama is a root vegetable with a water chestnut-type texture. Peel the thin, brown skin of this Mexican potato just before use.

1 cup finely chopped cooked chicken breast
½ cup chopped jicama
½ cup (2 ounces) shredded reduced-fat Cheddar cheese
¼ cup nonfat mayonnaise
1 tablespoon diced pimiento, drained
1 (4-ounce) can chopped green chiles, drained
6 (6-inch) corn tortillas

Combine first 6 ingredients in a small bowl; stir well. Set aside.

Cut each tortilla into 6 circles using a 2-inch biscuit cutter. Place tortilla chips on an ungreased baking sheet. Bake at 350° for 6 minutes. Turn chips, and bake an additional 2 to 3 minutes or until golden and crisp.

Spread chicken mixture evenly over chips (about 1 tablespoon per chip). Broil 5½ inches from heat (with electric oven door partially opened) 3 minutes or until hot and bubbly. Serve warm. Yield: 3 dozen appetizers.

Per Appetizer: 24 Calories (19% from Fat)
Fat 0.5g (Saturated Fat 0.2g)
Protein 1.9g Carbohydrate 2.8g
Cholesterol 4mg Sodium 38mg

Miniature Chicken Tostadas

Parmesan-Garlic Bagel Chips

These flavorful bagel chips are lower in fat than many commercial ones because they aren't heavily coated with oil or shortening before baking.

4 (2.5-ounce) plain bagels
Butter-flavored vegetable cooking spray
¼ cup grated Parmesan cheese
1½ teaspoons dried Italian seasoning
½ teaspoon garlic powder

Cut each bagel into 2 half-circles using a serrated knife. Cut each half-circle horizontally into ¼-inch-thick slices. Place slices on a wire rack; place rack on a baking sheet. Coat slices with cooking spray.

Combine cheese, Italian seasoning, and garlic powder; sprinkle evenly over bagel slices. Bake at 325° for 12 to 15 minutes or until lightly browned and crisp; let cool. Store in an airtight container. Yield: 4 dozen chips.

Per Chip: 19 Calories (14% from Fat)
Fat 0.3g (Saturated Fat 0.1g)
Protein 0.8g Carbohydrate 3.2g
Cholesterol 0mg Sodium 39mg

Honey-Sesame Snack

1 (8-inch) flour tortilla, quartered
1½ teaspoons honey
1½ teaspoons sesame seeds, toasted

Place tortilla wedges on an ungreased baking sheet; bake at 400° for 3 minutes. Brush each with honey; sprinkle with sesame seeds. Bake an additional 2 minutes or until golden. Yield: 4 wedges.

Per Snack: 48 Calories (24% from Fat)
Fat 1.3g (Saturated Fat 0.2g)
Protein 1.2g Carbohydrate 8.2g
Cholesterol 0mg Sodium 51mg

Spicy Snack Mix

1½ cups bite-size crispy corn cereal squares
1½ cups bite-size crispy rice cereal squares
1½ cups bite-size crispy wheat cereal squares
¾ cup small unsalted pretzels
¼ cup unsalted dry roasted peanuts
¼ cup nonfat margarine, melted
2 tablespoons low-sodium soy sauce
1½ teaspoons chili powder
½ teaspoon garlic powder
¼ teaspoon ground red pepper

Combine first 5 ingredients in a large heavy-duty, zip-top plastic bag.

Combine margarine and remaining ingredients; pour over cereal mixture. Seal bag, and shake well to coat.

Place cereal mixture in a 15- x 10- x 1-inch jelly-roll pan. Bake at 300° for 18 to 20 minutes, stirring occasionally. Remove from oven; let snack mix cool completely. Store in an airtight container. Yield: 10 (½-cup) servings.

Per Serving: 59 Calories (9% from Fat)
Fat 0.6g (Saturated Fat 0.1g)
Protein 1.3g Carbohydrate 11.6g
Cholesterol 0mg Sodium 223mg

Peach Pops

1 cup unsweetened pineapple juice
3 tablespoons powdered sugar
1 (8-ounce) container peach low-fat yogurt

Combine all ingredients; stir well. Spoon mixture evenly into 10 frozen-pop molds or (3-ounce) paper cups; insert wooden sticks. Freeze until firm. Yield: 10 pops.

Per Pop: 45 Calories (6% from Fat)
Fat 0.3g (Saturated Fat 0.2g)
Protein 1.0g Carbohydrate 9.9g
Cholesterol 1mg Sodium 12mg

Spicy Snack Mix

Melon-Lime Cooler and Citrus-Mint Cooler

Citrus-Mint Cooler

You may want to substitute other flavors of unsweetened sparkling water for a different twist.

1 cup loosely packed fresh mint leaves
2 cups unsweetened pink grapefruit juice
1 cup unsweetened orange juice
⅓ cup sugar
1 cup lemon-flavored sparkling water, chilled
Fresh mint sprigs (optional)

Combine first 4 ingredients in a medium bowl, stirring well. Cover and chill at least 8 hours, stirring occasionally. Pour mixture through a wire-mesh strainer into a pitcher, discarding mint. Just before serving, stir in sparkling water. Garnish with mint sprigs, if desired. Yield: 4 (1-cup) servings.

Per Serving: 139 Calories (1% from Fat)
Fat 0.2g (Saturated Fat 0.0g)
Protein 1.0g Carbohydrate 34.3g
Cholesterol 0mg Sodium 14mg

Melon-Lime Cooler

4½ cups cubed honeydew melon (about 1 small)
1½ cups lime sherbet
2 tablespoons lime juice
Fresh strawberries (optional)

Place melon cubes in a single layer on a baking sheet. Cover and freeze 30 minutes or until firm.

Position knife blade in food processor bowl; add frozen melon, sherbet, and lime juice. Process until smooth. Pour into glasses. Garnish with strawberries, if desired. Serve immediately. Yield: 5 (1-cup) servings.

Per Serving: 131 Calories (5% from Fat)
Fat 0.7g (Saturated Fat 0.4g)
Protein 1.5g Carbohydrate 32.4g
Cholesterol 0mg Sodium 59mg

Mock Margaritas

(pictured on page 28)

1 (6-ounce) can frozen lemonade concentrate, thawed and undiluted
1 (6-ounce) can frozen limeade concentrate, thawed and undiluted
½ cup sifted powdered sugar
3¼ cups crushed ice
1½ cups club soda, chilled
Lime slices (optional)

Combine lemonade and limeade concentrates, powdered sugar, and crushed ice in a large plastic container; stir well. Freeze mixture. Remove from freezer 30 minutes before serving.

Spoon mixture into container of an electric blender; add club soda. Cover and process until smooth. Pour into glasses; garnish with lime slices, if desired. Yield: 6 (1-cup) servings.

Per Serving: 143 Calories (1% from Fat)
Fat 0.1g (Saturated Fat 0.0g)
Protein 0.1g Carbohydrate 37.3g
Cholesterol 0mg Sodium 13mg

Ruby Refresher

1 (16-ounce) bag unsweetened frozen strawberries
1 (12-ounce) can frozen cranberry juice cocktail concentrate, thawed and undiluted
1 cup unsweetened pineapple juice, chilled
¼ cup lemon juice, chilled
2½ cups club soda, chilled

Combine strawberries and cranberry juice concentrate in container of an electric blender or food processor; cover and process until smooth. Transfer mixture to a large pitcher; stir in pineapple juice and lemon juice. Stir in club soda just before serving. Serve immediately. Yield: 8 (1-cup) servings.

Per Serving: 189 Calories (1% from Fat)
Fat 0.2g (Saturated Fat 0.0g)
Protein 0.4g Carbohydrate 48.6g
Cholesterol 0mg Sodium 27mg

Peach Delight

1½ cups peach nectar, chilled
2 (16-ounce) cans peach slices in juice, drained
1 (8-ounce) carton vanilla low-fat yogurt
⅛ teaspoon almond extract

Combine all ingredients in container of an electric blender; cover and process until smooth. Pour into glasses, and serve immediately. Yield: 5 (1-cup) servings.

Per Serving: 109 Calories (7% from Fat)
Fat 0.8g (Saturated Fat 0.4g)
Protein 3.0g Carbohydrate 24.3g
Cholesterol 2mg Sodium 39mg

Amaretto Smoothie

3 cups low-fat strawberry ice cream, softened
1 cup skim milk
⅓ cup amaretto
Whole fresh strawberries (optional)

Combine first 3 ingredients in container of an electric blender; cover and process until smooth. Pour into champagne glasses, and garnish with whole strawberries, if desired. Serve immediately. Yield: 6 (⅔-cup) servings.

Per Serving: 135 Calories (14% from Fat)
Fat 2.1g (Saturated Fat 1.1g)
Protein 3.4g Carbohydrate 19.7g
Cholesterol 11mg Sodium 66mg

Peanutty Banana Shake

Use ripe bananas for this refreshing milkshake.

1 cup peeled, sliced banana (about 1 large)
2 cups skim milk
1 tablespoon creamy peanut butter
1 tablespoon honey

Place banana slices in a single layer on a baking sheet. Cover and freeze until firm. Place milk in a shallow container; cover and freeze 45 minutes or until milk is slushy.

Combine frozen banana, milk, peanut butter, and honey in container of an electric blender; cover and process until smooth. Serve immediately. Yield: 3 (1-cup) servings.

Per Serving: 160 Calories (19% from Fat)
Fat 3.3g (Saturated Fat 0.8g)
Protein 7.6g Carbohydrate 27.3g
Cholesterol 3mg Sodium 112mg

Piña Coladas

1 (8-ounce) can pineapple chunks in juice, undrained
1 large ripe banana, peeled and sliced
1 (12-ounce) can evaporated skimmed milk, chilled
¼ cup light rum
½ teaspoon coconut extract
Ice cubes

Combine half of each of first 5 ingredients in container of an electric blender; cover and process until smooth. Gradually add enough ice cubes to bring mixture to 3-cup level; process until smooth.

Transfer to a pitcher. Repeat procedure with remaining ingredients. Serve immediately. Yield: 6 (1-cup) servings.

Per Serving: 115 Calories (2% from Fat)
Fat 0.3g (Saturated Fat 0.1g)
Protein 4.7g Carbohydrate 17.4g
Cholesterol 2mg Sodium 66mg

From left: *Apricot-Melon Freeze, Amaretto Smoothie, and Sparkling Punch*

Apricot-Melon Freeze

1 (16-ounce) package frozen cantaloupe and honeydew melon balls
1 (12-ounce) can apricot nectar
1 (10-ounce) bottle club soda, chilled
1 cup ice cubes
¼ teaspoon rum extract

Combine frozen cantaloupe and honeydew melon balls and apricot nectar in container of an electric blender; cover and process melon mixture until smooth. Add chilled club soda, ice cubes, and rum extract to melon mixture; process until smooth. Pour beverage into glasses, and serve immediately. Yield: 6 (1-cup) servings.

Per Serving: 59 Calories (3% from Fat)
Fat 0.2g (Saturated Fat 0.1g)
Protein 0.7g Carbohydrate 14.8g
Cholesterol 0mg Sodium 19mg

Sparkling Punch

3 cups chopped fresh pineapple (about 1½ pounds)
2 cups unsweetened pineapple-orange-banana juice
4 cups lime-flavored sparkling mineral water, chilled
2 cups Chablis or other dry white wine, chilled

Combine pineapple and juice in container of an electric blender; cover and process until smooth. Pour mixture into a 13- x 9- x 2-inch pan. Cover and freeze until firm.

Partially thaw fruit mixture; break into chunks, and place in a punch bowl. Add mineral water and wine; stir until slushy. Yield: 12 (1-cup) servings.

Per Serving: 77 Calories (3% from Fat)
Fat 0.3g (Saturated Fat 0.0g)
Protein 0.3g Carbohydrate 13.0g
Cholesterol 0mg Sodium 21mg

Frosted Cappuccino

This combination of nonfat ingredients creates the sweet taste and texture of a sinfully rich coffee beverage.

2 cups brewed espresso coffee, chilled
2 cups vanilla nonfat ice cream
½ teaspoon vanilla extract
Ground cinnamon (optional)

Combine first 3 ingredients in container of an electric blender; cover and process until smooth. Pour into glasses. Sprinkle each serving with cinnamon, if desired. Serve immediately. Yield: 4 (1-cup) servings.

Per Serving: 104 Calories (0% from Fat)
Fat 0.0g (Saturated Fat 0.0g)
Protein 2.1g Carbohydrate 22.7g
Cholesterol 0mg Sodium 47mg

Hot Cranberry Cider

1 quart unsweetened apple cider
2 cups cranberry juice cocktail
1 teaspoon whole cloves
1 (3-inch) stick cinnamon

Combine all ingredients in a large saucepan; bring to a boil. Reduce heat, and simmer 10 minutes. Discard spices; serve warm. Yield: 6 (1-cup) servings.

Per Serving: 129 Calories (2% from Fat)
Fat 0.3g (Saturated Fat 0.1g)
Protein 0.1g Carbohydrate 32.3g
Cholesterol 0mg Sodium 9mg

Hot Cocoa Mix

1¾ cups instant nonfat dry milk powder
1 cup sifted powdered sugar
⅔ cup miniature marshmallows
½ cup unsweetened cocoa
½ teaspoon ground cinnamon

Combine all ingredients; stir well. Store in an airtight container. To serve, spoon 3 tablespoons cocoa mix into each mug. Add ¾ cup hot water to each; stir well. Yield: 16 (1-cup) servings.

Per Serving: 95 Calories (5% from Fat)
Fat 0.5g (Saturated Fat 0.3g)
Protein 5.6g Carbohydrate 17.2g
Cholesterol 3mg Sodium 72mg

Minted Hot Cocoa Mix

Omit marshmallows and cinnamon, and add 4 (4½-inch) sticks of peppermint candy, crushed, to Hot Cocoa Mix. Yield: 14 (1-cup) servings.

Per Serving: 105 Calories (4% from Fat)
Fat 0.5g (Saturated Fat 0.3g)
Protein 6.3g Carbohydrate 18.8g
Cholesterol 3mg Sodium 82mg

Mocha-Cocoa Mix

Omit marshmallows, and add ¼ cup instant coffee granules to Hot Cocoa Mix. Yield: 14 (1-cup) servings.

Per Serving: 105 Calories (5% from Fat)
Fat 0.6g (Saturated Fat 0.3g)
Protein 6.5g Carbohydrate 18.7g
Cholesterol 3mg Sodium 82mg

Gift from the Kitchen

Welcome new neighbors with a delicious and healthy gift from your kitchen—a decorative jar filled with Hot Cocoa Mix. Pack the mix in a basket, perhaps with one or two unique mugs. Be sure to include the recipe that gives directions for storing the mix as well as instructions for use.

Hot Cocoa Mix

HURRY-UP BREADS

Are dinner rolls and frozen waffles always on your grocery list? With only a bit more time, you can make your own quick breads, such as Southern Cornbread on page 55. It takes only 30 minutes to prepare and will be a welcome addition to family suppers. For breakfast, Blueberry-Yogurt Muffins (page 48) are a quick morning fix.

Be sure to try all three of the breadstick versions on page 56. They make use of hot roll mix—a convenient way to enjoy the flavor of homemade yeast bread.

Clockwise from bottom: *Parmesan Breadsticks, Orange-Glazed Breadsticks, and Cinnamon Breadsticks (recipes on page 56)*

Cinnamon-Raisin Biscuits

Cinnamon-Raisin Biscuits

Remember that overmixing the batter can cause biscuits or muffins to be tough.

2 cups all-purpose flour
2 teaspoons baking powder
¼ teaspoon salt
½ teaspoon ground cinnamon
1½ tablespoons sugar
3 tablespoons chilled stick margarine, cut into small pieces
½ cup raisins
¾ cup 1% low-fat milk
½ cup sifted powdered sugar
1 tablespoon 1% low-fat milk

Combine first 5 ingredients in a bowl; cut in margarine with a pastry blender until mixture resembles coarse meal. Add raisins; toss well. Add ¾ cup milk; stir just until dry ingredients are moistened.

Turn dough out onto a heavily floured surface; knead dough 4 or 5 times. Roll dough to ½-inch thickness; cut with a 2½-inch biscuit cutter. Place on a baking sheet. Bake at 450° for 11 minutes or until golden.

Combine powdered sugar and 1 tablespoon milk; stir well. Drizzle over hot biscuits. Yield: 1 dozen.

PER BISCUIT: 153 CALORIES (19% FROM FAT)
FAT 3.3G (SATURATED FAT 0.7G)
PROTEIN 2.9G CARBOHYDRATE 28.2G
CHOLESTEROL 1MG SODIUM 142MG

Buttermilk Biscuits

2 cups all-purpose flour
2 teaspoons baking powder
½ teaspoon baking soda
¼ teaspoon salt
1 tablespoon sugar
¼ cup reduced-calorie stick margarine
¾ cup plus 1 tablespoon nonfat buttermilk
Vegetable cooking spray

Combine first 5 ingredients in a medium bowl; cut in margarine with a pastry blender until mixture resembles coarse meal. Add buttermilk, stirring just until dry ingredients are moistened.

Turn dough out onto a lightly floured surface, and knead 5 or 6 times. Roll dough to ½-inch thickness; cut into rounds with a 2½-inch biscuit cutter. Place rounds on a baking sheet coated with cooking spray. Bake at 425° for 10 to 12 minutes or until biscuits are golden. Yield: 8 biscuits.

PER BISCUIT: 163 CALORIES (23% FROM FAT)
FAT 4.1G (SATURATED FAT 0.6G)
PROTEIN 4.2G CARBOHYDRATE 27.3G
CHOLESTEROL 1MG SODIUM 282MG

Orange Drop Biscuits

1¼ cups all-purpose flour
1½ teaspoons baking powder
¼ teaspoon baking soda
1 tablespoon sugar
3 tablespoons reduced-calorie stick margarine
⅓ cup 1% low-fat cottage cheese
¼ cup frozen egg substitute, thawed
3 tablespoons low-sugar orange marmalade
¾ teaspoon grated orange rind
Vegetable cooking spray

Combine first 4 ingredients; cut in margarine with pastry blender until mixture resembles coarse meal. Combine cottage cheese, egg substitute, orange marmalade, and orange rind; add to flour mixture, stirring just until dry ingredients are moistened.

Drop dough by tablespoonfuls onto a baking sheet coated with cooking spray. Bake at 400° for 8 minutes or until golden. Yield: 20 biscuits.

PER BISCUIT: 45 CALORIES (24% FROM FAT)
FAT 1.2G (SATURATED FAT 0.2G)
PROTEIN 1.6G CARBOHYDRATE 7.0G
CHOLESTEROL 0MG SODIUM 70MG

Peanut Butter and Jelly Muffins

2 cups all-purpose flour
2 teaspoons baking powder
1/8 teaspoon salt
1/3 cup firmly packed brown sugar
1/3 cup creamy peanut butter
1 egg, beaten
1 cup skim milk
Vegetable cooking spray
2 tablespoons low-sugar grape spread

Combine first 4 ingredients in a bowl; make a well in center of mixture, and set aside. Combine peanut butter and egg in a bowl; beat at low speed of an electric mixer until blended. Add peanut butter mixture and milk to flour mixture, stirring just until dry ingredients are moistened.

Spoon batter into muffin pans coated with cooking spray, filling half full. Top each with 1/2 teaspoon grape spread, and top with remaining batter. Bake at 425° for 16 minutes or until golden. Remove from pans immediately; cool on wire racks. Yield: 1 dozen.

Per Muffin: 158 Calories (25% from Fat)
Fat 4.4g (Saturated Fat 0.8g)
Protein 5.4g Carbohydrate 24.8g
Cholesterol 19mg Sodium 76mg

Lemon-Prune Muffins

1 1/2 cups all-purpose flour
1/2 cup whole wheat flour
1 teaspoon baking powder
1 teaspoon baking soda
1/4 teaspoon salt
1/3 cup firmly packed brown sugar
3/4 cup plain nonfat yogurt
1/2 cup chopped pitted prunes
2 tablespoons margarine, melted
1 tablespoon grated lemon rind
2 tablespoons fresh lemon juice
1 egg
Vegetable cooking spray

Combine first 6 ingredients in a large bowl; make a well in center of mixture. Combine yogurt and next 5 ingredients in a bowl; stir well. Add to dry ingredients, stirring just until moistened.

Divide batter among 12 muffin pans coated with cooking spray. Bake at 400° for 15 minutes or until a wooden pick inserted in center comes out clean. Remove from pans immediately; let cool on a wire rack. Yield: 1 dozen.

Per Muffin: 151 Calories (17% from Fat)
Fat 2.9g (Saturated Fat 0.6g)
Protein 3.9g Carbohydrate 28.3g
Cholesterol 19mg Sodium 196mg

Blueberry-Yogurt Muffins

2 cups all-purpose flour
1 teaspoon baking powder
1 teaspoon baking soda
1/4 teaspoon salt
1/3 cup sugar
1/4 cup unsweetened orange juice
2 tablespoons vegetable oil
1 teaspoon vanilla extract
1 (8-ounce) carton vanilla low-fat yogurt
1 egg
1 cup fresh or frozen blueberries, thawed
Vegetable cooking spray
1 tablespoon sugar

Combine first 5 ingredients in a large bowl; make a well in center of mixture. Combine orange juice and next 4 ingredients; stir well. Add to dry ingredients, stirring just until moistened. Gently fold in blueberries.

Divide batter among 12 muffin pans coated with cooking spray; sprinkle 1 tablespoon sugar evenly over muffins. Bake at 400° for 18 minutes or until golden. Remove from pans immediately; let cool on a wire rack. Yield: 1 dozen.

Per Muffin: 156 Calories (20% from Fat)
Fat 3.4g (Saturated Fat 0.7g)
Protein 3.7g Carbohydrate 27.6g
Cholesterol 19mg Sodium 173mg

Make a well in center of mixture.

Add liquid ingredients to dry ingredients.

Stir until dry ingredients are moistened.

Gently fold in blueberries.

Blueberry Yogurt Muffins

Overnight Bran Muffins

Overnight Bran Muffins

4 cups wheat bran flakes cereal with raisins
2½ cups all-purpose flour
1 cup mixed dried fruit
1½ teaspoons baking soda
1 teaspoon salt
⅔ cup sugar
2 cups nonfat buttermilk
2 eggs, lightly beaten
¼ cup vegetable oil
Vegetable cooking spray

Combine cereal, flour, dried fruit, baking soda, salt, and sugar in a large bowl; make a well in the center of cereal mixture.

Combine buttermilk, eggs, and oil; add to dry ingredients, stirring just until moistened. Cover tightly, and chill at least 12 hours.

Divide batter evenly among 24 (2½-inch) muffin pans coated with cooking spray. Bake at 400° for 14 to 15 minutes or until muffins are lightly browned. Yield: 2 dozen.

Note: Muffin batter will keep in refrigerator up to 3 days.

Per Muffin: 160 Calories (20% from Fat)
Fat 3.5g (Saturated Fat 0.6g)
Protein 3.6g Carbohydrate 29.6g
Cholesterol 21mg Sodium 272mg

Amaretto French Toast

You may use 2 tablespoons additional milk and 1/4 teaspoon almond extract instead of the amaretto.

2 egg whites
1/3 cup skim milk
2 tablespoons brown sugar
3 tablespoons frozen egg substitute, thawed
2 tablespoons amaretto
1/4 teaspoon salt
1/4 teaspoon ground cinnamon
8 (3/4-inch-thick) slices French bread
Vegetable cooking spray

Beat egg whites at high speed of an electric mixer until stiff peaks form. Set aside.

Combine milk and next 5 ingredients in a medium bowl, beating at high speed of an electric mixer until smooth. Gently fold one-third of egg whites into milk mixture; fold in remaining whites.

Dip bread slices in milk mixture; place in a 13- x 9- x 2-inch baking pan coated with cooking spray. Bake at 425° for 7 minutes; turn and bake an additional 3 minutes or until golden. Yield: 8 servings.

Per Serving: 114 Calories (6% from Fat)
Fat 0.7g (Saturated Fat 0.2g)
Protein 4.3g Carbohydrate 19.7g
Cholesterol 1mg Sodium 265mg

Orange Scones

2 cups all-purpose flour
2 teaspoons baking powder
1/2 teaspoon baking soda
1/4 teaspoon salt
1/3 cup sugar
3 tablespoons chilled stick margarine, cut into small pieces
1 (8-ounce) carton lemon low-fat yogurt
2 teaspoons grated orange rind
1/4 cup unsweetened orange juice
Vegetable cooking spray
1 tablespoon sugar

Combine first 5 ingredients in a bowl; cut in margarine with a pastry blender until mixture resembles coarse meal. Add yogurt, orange rind, and orange juice to dry ingredients, stirring just until moistened. (Dough will be sticky.)

With floured hands, pat dough into a 9-inch circle on a baking sheet coated with cooking spray. Cut into 10 wedges, cutting into but not through dough. Sprinkle with 1 tablespoon sugar. Bake at 400° for 16 minutes or until golden. Yield: 10 scones.

Per Scone: 180 Calories (20% from Fat)
Fat 3.9g (Saturated Fat 0.7g)
Protein 3.3g Carbohydrate 33.0g
Cholesterol 0mg Sodium 215mg

Yogurt Waffles

2 cups all-purpose flour
1 teaspoon baking soda
1/2 teaspoon baking powder
1/4 teaspoon salt
1 tablespoon sugar
1 1/2 cups skim milk
3/4 cup plain nonfat yogurt
2 tablespoons vegetable oil
3 egg whites
1/8 teaspoon cream of tartar
Vegetable cooking spray

Combine first 5 ingredients in a large bowl; make a well in center of mixture. Combine milk, yogurt, and oil; stir with a wire whisk. Add to dry ingredients, stirring just until moistened.

Beat egg whites and cream of tartar at high speed of an electric mixer until stiff peaks form; gently fold beaten egg white mixture into batter.

Coat an 8-inch square waffle iron with cooking spray; allow waffle iron to preheat. For each waffle, spoon 1 1/4 cups batter onto hot waffle iron, spreading batter to edges. Bake 4 to 5 minutes or until steaming stops. Repeat procedure with remaining batter. Yield: 16 (4-inch) waffles.

Per Waffle: 93 Calories (19% from Fat)
Fat 2.0g (Saturated Fat 0.4g)
Protein 3.6g Carbohydrate 14.8g
Cholesterol 1mg Sodium 129mg

Banana Pancakes

1 cup all-purpose flour
1/8 teaspoon salt
1 tablespoon sugar
1 cup nonfat buttermilk
1 teaspoon baking soda
1/2 cup mashed ripe banana
1/2 cup frozen egg substitute, thawed
1 tablespoon vegetable oil
Vegetable cooking spray

Combine first 3 ingredients in a large bowl; make a well in center of mixture. Combine buttermilk and soda, stirring well. Add banana, egg substitute, and oil; stir well. Add buttermilk mixture to dry ingredients, stirring just until moistened.

Coat a nonstick griddle with cooking spray; preheat to 350°. For each pancake, pour 1/4 cup batter onto hot griddle. Cook pancakes until tops are covered with bubbles and edges look cooked; turn and cook other side. Yield: 12 (4-inch) pancakes.

Per Pancake: 75 Calories (17% from Fat)
Fat 1.4g (Saturated Fat 0.3g)
Protein 2.9g Carbohydrate 12.6g
Cholesterol 1mg Sodium 130mg

Shredded Wheat Pancakes

You won't miss the margarine or syrup when you top pancakes with Strawberry Sauce.

3/4 cup all-purpose flour
1/2 cup crushed shredded whole wheat cereal biscuits
1 tablespoon baking powder
1/4 teaspoon salt
2 teaspoons sugar
1 egg, beaten
1 cup skim milk
1 tablespoon vegetable oil
Vegetable cooking spray
Strawberry Sauce

Combine first 5 ingredients in a medium bowl; make a well in center of mixture. Combine egg, milk, and oil; add to dry ingredients, stirring just until moistened.

For each pancake, pour 1/4 cup batter onto a hot griddle coated with cooking spray. Turn pancakes when the tops are covered with bubbles and edges look cooked. To serve, top each pancake with 1/4 cup Strawberry Sauce. Yield: 8 servings.

Strawberry Sauce

3 cups fresh strawberries, sliced
2 1/2 tablespoons sugar
2 1/2 teaspoons cornstarch
1/4 teaspoon almond extract

Combine strawberries and sugar; cover and chill 6 to 8 hours. Drain strawberries, reserving juice; set aside.

Add enough water to strawberry juice to make 3/4 cup. Combine juice and cornstarch in a saucepan, stirring until cornstarch is dissolved. Cook over medium heat, stirring constantly, until smooth and thickened. Stir in strawberries and almond extract. Serve warm or chilled. Yield: 2 cups.

Per Serving: 129 Calories (20% from Fat)
Fat 2.9g (Saturated Fat 0.6g)
Protein 3.7g Carbohydrate 22.7g
Cholesterol 28mg Sodium 99mg

FYI

When preparing breads, cakes, or cookies, it's important to measure flour accurately. Unless specified, you don't need to sift all-purpose flour before measuring. Just stir the flour lightly, and then spoon it into a dry-ingredient measuring cup. Use the straight edge of a knife or spatula to level, and avoid shaking the cup as this will pack the flour.

Shredded Wheat Pancakes

Mexican Corn Sticks

Mexican Corn Sticks

To keep the cheese from sticking to the pans, coat the pans lightly with cooking spray, and don't preheat them before filling with batter.

1¼ cups all-purpose flour
¾ cup yellow cornmeal
2 teaspoons baking powder
1 teaspoon baking soda
¼ teaspoon salt
Dash of ground red pepper
¾ cup nonfat buttermilk
1 (8¾-ounce) can no-salt-added cream-style corn
1 (4-ounce) can chopped green chiles, undrained
2 egg whites, lightly beaten
½ cup (2 ounces) shredded reduced-fat sharp Cheddar cheese
Vegetable cooking spray

Combine first 6 ingredients in a medium bowl; make a well in center of mixture. Combine buttermilk and next 3 ingredients; add to dry ingredients, stirring until moistened. Fold in cheese.

Spoon batter into cast-iron cactus-shaped or traditional corn stick pans coated with cooking spray, filling two-thirds full. Bake at 425° for 18 to 20 minutes or until golden. Remove from pans immediately. Yield: 16 corn sticks.

Per Corn Stick: 91 Calories (12% from Fat)
Fat 1.2g (Saturated Fat 0.5g)
Protein 3.8g Carbohydrate 16.7g
Cholesterol 3mg Sodium 194mg

Quick Tip

To add flavor to commercial French bread, cut lengthwise and coat cut sides with butter-flavored cooking spray. Sprinkle with sesame seeds, chopped fresh herbs, or minced onion, and place under a broiler until toasted.

Southern Cornbread

1 cup all-purpose flour
¾ cup yellow cornmeal
2 teaspoons baking powder
¾ teaspoon salt
2 tablespoons sugar
1 cup skim milk
2 tablespoons vegetable oil
1 egg
Vegetable cooking spray

Combine first 5 ingredients in a bowl; make a well in center of mixture. Combine milk, oil, and egg; stir well. Add to dry ingredients, stirring until moistened.

Spoon batter into an 8-inch square baking pan coated with cooking spray. Bake at 425° for 20 minutes or until done. Let cool 5 minutes in pan on a wire rack before serving. Yield: 9 servings.

Per Serving: 150 Calories (25% from Fat)
Fat 4.1g (Saturated Fat 0.8g)
Protein 4.1g Carbohydrate 23.9g
Cholesterol 25mg Sodium 284mg

Cheesy Garlic Bread

1 (1-pound) loaf Italian bread
Butter-flavored vegetable cooking spray
¼ cup freshly grated Parmesan cheese
1 tablespoon minced fresh parsley
¼ teaspoon garlic powder

Slice bread in half lengthwise; coat cut surface of each half with cooking spray. Combine cheese, parsley, and garlic powder; sprinkle over cut surface of one half of bread. Top with other half of bread.

Wrap bread in aluminum foil; bake at 350° for 20 minutes or until bread is thoroughly heated. Yield: 20 (½-inch-thick) slices.

Per Slice: 69 Calories (8% from Fat)
Fat 0.6g (Saturated Fat 0.4g)
Protein 2.6g Carbohydrate 12.9g
Cholesterol 1mg Sodium 156mg

Parmesan Breadsticks

(pictured on page 44)

1 (16-ounce) package hot roll mix
1/4 cup grated Parmesan cheese
1 teaspoon dried Italian seasoning
1 cup hot water (120° to 130°)
1 egg white, lightly beaten
2 tablespoons vegetable oil
Butter-flavored vegetable cooking spray
2 tablespoons plus 2 teaspoons grated Parmesan cheese

Combine roll mix, yeast from packet, 1/4 cup cheese, and Italian seasoning in a large bowl. Add hot water, egg white, and oil; stir until moistened. Shape into a ball.

Turn out dough onto a lightly floured surface. Knead until smooth and elastic (about 5 minutes). Cover and let rest 5 minutes.

Roll dough into a 16- x 12-inch rectangle on a lightly floured surface. Cut rectangle crosswise with a pastry cutter to form 16 strips. Cut strips in half to form 32 (6-inch) strips. Twist each strip 5 or 6 times, and place on baking sheets coated with cooking spray.

Spray tops of strips with cooking spray; sprinkle each strip with 1/4 teaspoon cheese. Cover and let rise in a warm place (about 85°), free from drafts, 20 to 30 minutes or until doubled in bulk. Bake at 375° for 12 to 14 minutes or until golden. Yield: 32 breadsticks.

Per Breadstick: 63 Calories (17% from Fat)
Fat 1.2g (Saturated Fat 0.4g)
Protein 2.0g Carbohydrate 10.6g
Cholesterol 1mg Sodium 121mg

Cinnamon Breadsticks

Follow directions for Parmesan Breadsticks, omitting cheese and Italian seasoning. Place dough strips on baking sheets coated with cooking spray; brush strips with 1/4 cup reduced-calorie stick margarine, melted. Combine 1/4 cup sugar and 3/4 teaspoon ground cinnamon, and sprinkle over dough strips. Let rise, and bake as directed for Parmesan Breadsticks. Yield: 32 breadsticks.

Per Breadstick: 71 Calories (23% from Fat)
Fat 1.8g (Saturated Fat 0.2g)
Protein 1.6g Carbohydrate 11.7g
Cholesterol 0mg Sodium 115mg

Orange-Glazed Breadsticks

Follow directions for Parmesan Breadsticks, omitting cheese and Italian seasoning and adding 1 tablespoon grated orange rind to dough. Place dough strips on baking sheets coated with cooking spray; spray tops of strips with cooking spray. Let rise; bake as directed for Parmesan Breadsticks.

Combine 1 1/4 cups sifted powdered sugar, 1 1/2 tablespoons skim milk, and 1/4 teaspoon orange extract. Drizzle over hot breadsticks. Yield: 32 breadsticks.

Per Serving: 77 Calories (11% from Fat)
Fat 0.9g (Saturated Fat 0.2g)
Protein 1.6g Carbohydrate 15.2g
Cholesterol 0mg Sodium 102mg

Cinnamon Crisps

Combine sugar and cinnamon in an empty salt shaker to coat the tortillas evenly.

1 tablespoon hot water
1/2 teaspoon vanilla extract
1 1/2 tablespoons sugar
1 teaspoon ground cinnamon
4 (6-inch) flour tortillas
Vegetable cooking spray

Combine water and vanilla in a small bowl; stir well. Combine sugar and cinnamon; stir well. Lightly coat both sides of 2 tortillas with cooking spray; lightly brush each side with water mixture, and sprinkle each side with sugar mixture.

Place on a wire rack in a 15- x 10- x 1-inch jellyroll pan. Bake at 400° for 6 1/2 minutes or until lightly browned. Repeat procedure for remaining 2 tortillas. Yield: 4 servings.

Per Serving: 136 Calories (18% from Fat)
Fat 2.7g (Saturated Fat 0.4g)
Protein 3.1g Carbohydrate 24.7g
Cholesterol 0mg Sodium 168mg

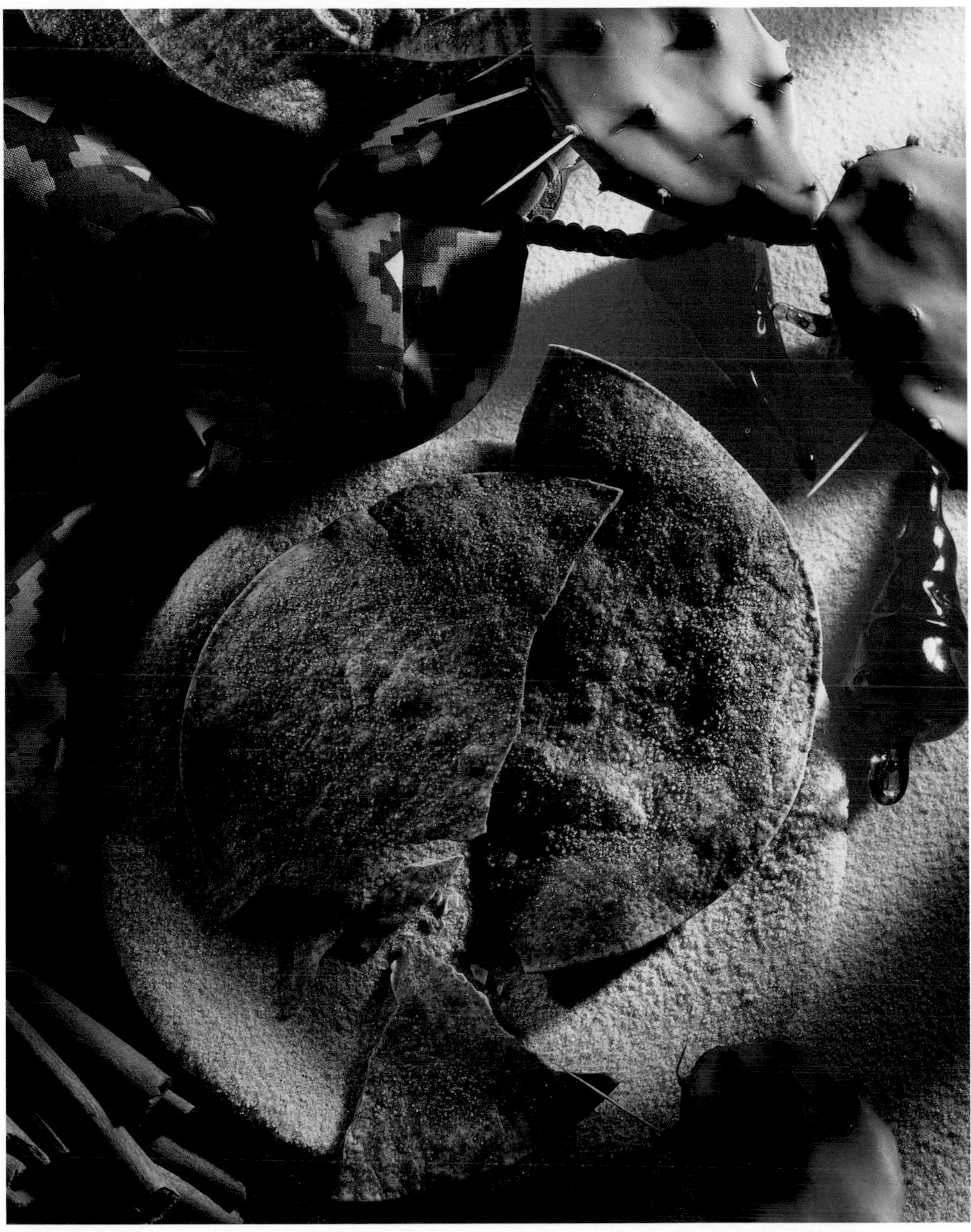

Cinnamon Crisps

TIME-SAVING ENTRÉES

Simplify meals by starting with a quick entrée. If your family members are strictly meat-and-potato fans, turn to our Vegetable-Beef Pot Pie (page 61). It calls for refrigerated roll dough to keep preparation time to a minimum. When you expect guests for dinner, try elegant Veal Piccata (page 62) or Minted Lamb Chops (page 67).

One of the best time-saving hints for many entrées is to double a recipe so that the extra servings can be frozen for later use. Italian Meat Sauce (page 61) and Chicken Vermicelli (page 67) are both excellent make-and-freeze choices.

Hoisin Pork Medaillons *(recipe on page 64)*

Italian Meat Sauce

Italian Meat Sauce

1½ pounds ground round
2 cups sliced fresh mushrooms
½ cup chopped onion
2 large cloves garlic, minced
¼ cup Burgundy or other dry red wine
2 teaspoons dried Italian seasoning
¼ teaspoon salt
¼ teaspoon black pepper
⅛ teaspoon ground red pepper
1 (28-ounce) can tomato puree

Crumble beef into a microwave-safe colander; set colander in a glass pieplate. Microwave, uncovered, at HIGH 8 to 9 minutes or until browned, stirring every 3 minutes; set aside. Discard drippings.

Combine mushrooms, onion, and garlic in a 3-quart casserole. Cover with wax paper, and microwave at HIGH 5 to 6 minutes or until onion is tender. Add beef, wine, and remaining ingredients to casserole, stirring well. Cover and microwave at HIGH 6 minutes or until thoroughly heated, stirring once. Serve over hot cooked pasta. Yield: 8 (¾-cup) servings.

Per Serving: 176 Calories (28% from Fat)
Fat 5.4g (Saturated Fat 2.0g)
Protein 20.6g Carbohydrate 12.5g
Cholesterol 53mg Sodium 512mg

Microwave Magic

Here's how to tell whether or not a container is microwave-safe. Place a 1-cup glass measure filled with water in the microwave along with the container you are testing. Microwave at HIGH for 1 minute. If the dish remains cool, it is safe for microwaving. If it's slightly warm, it is probably safe for heating or reheating but not for cooking. If the dish is hot, do not use it in the microwave.

Vegetable-Beef Pot Pie

Purchase frozen chopped onion to save time, or chop and freeze your own.

Vegetable cooking spray
1 cup chopped onion
½ pound lean boneless sirloin steak, cut into 1-inch strips
1 cup peeled, cubed baking potato
1 (10-ounce) package frozen mixed vegetables
2 tablespoons cornstarch
2 cups canned no-salt-added beef broth, undiluted
½ teaspoon dried thyme
½ teaspoon dried basil
¼ teaspoon salt
¼ teaspoon pepper
1 (4-ounce) package refrigerated crescent dinner rolls

Coat a large nonstick skillet with cooking spray; place over medium heat until hot. Add onion and steak, and sauté 3 minutes or until onion is tender. Add potato and mixed vegetables; sauté 2 minutes.

Place cornstarch in a bowl. Gradually add broth, blending with a wire whisk; add to skillet. Stir in thyme and next 3 ingredients; bring to a boil over medium heat, stirring occasionally. Reduce heat, and simmer, uncovered, 15 minutes or until thickened. Spoon beef mixture into a 2-quart casserole coated with cooking spray; set aside.

Unroll dinner roll dough and separate into 2 rectangles; roll each portion to an 8- x 4-inch rectangle. Cut each rectangle lengthwise into 4 (1-inch) strips. Arrange strips in a lattice design over beef mixture. Bake at 375° for 20 minutes or until filling is bubbly and the lattice crust is golden. Yield: 4 (1-cup) servings.

Per Serving: 304 Calories (27% from Fat)
Fat 9.2g (Saturated Fat 2.4g)
Protein 18.0g Carbohydrate 35.8g
Cholesterol 35mg Sodium 436mg

Veal Piccata

Veal Piccata

1 pound veal cutlets (¼ inch thick)
¼ cup all-purpose flour
Vegetable cooking spray
1 teaspoon olive oil
½ cup dry sherry
¼ cup lemon juice
2 tablespoons capers
Lemon slices (optional)
Chopped fresh parsley (optional)

Trim fat from cutlets. Dredge cutlets in flour. Coat a large nonstick skillet with cooking spray; add oil. Place over medium-high heat until hot. Add veal, and cook 3 minutes on each side or until browned. Remove veal from skillet; drain and pat dry with paper towels. Transfer veal to a serving platter. Set aside; keep warm.

Add sherry, lemon juice, and capers to skillet; stir well, scraping bottom of pan to loosen brown bits. Cook over medium-high heat, stirring occasionally, until mixture is reduced by half. Pour sauce over veal. If desired, garnish with lemon slices and fresh parsley. Yield: 4 servings.

Per Serving: 178 Calories (24% from Fat)
Fat 4.6g (Saturated Fat 1.1g)
Protein 24.0g Carbohydrate 8.7g
Cholesterol 94mg Sodium 435mg

Veal Marsala

1 pound (¼-inch-thick) veal scaloppine
½ teaspoon dried rosemary, crushed
¼ teaspoon salt
¼ teaspoon freshly ground pepper
Vegetable cooking spray
1 teaspoon olive oil
2 cloves garlic, minced
2 cups quartered fresh mushrooms
1 teaspoon cornstarch
⅓ cup canned low-sodium chicken broth, undiluted
⅓ cup dry Marsala wine

Trim fat from veal. Sprinkle rosemary, salt, and pepper over both sides of veal; set aside.

Coat a large nonstick skillet with cooking spray; add oil. Place over medium-high heat until hot. Add garlic; sauté 30 seconds. Add half of veal, and cook 2 minutes on each side or until veal is lightly browned. Remove veal from skillet, and place on a serving platter; set aside, and keep warm. Repeat with remaining veal.

Add mushrooms to skillet, and sauté 3 minutes or until tender. Place cornstarch in a bowl. Gradually add broth, stirring with a wire whisk. Add cornstarch mixture and wine to skillet; cook 2 minutes or until thickened and bubbly, stirring constantly. Spoon sauce over veal. Yield: 4 servings.

Per Serving: 164 Calories (30% from Fat)
Fat 5.4g (Saturated Fat 1.4g)
Protein 23.9g Carbohydrate 3.9g
Cholesterol 91mg Sodium 260mg

Apricot-Glazed Ham

1 (2-pound) lean cooked, boneless ham, cut into 8 slices
Vegetable cooking spray
⅓ cup low-sugar apricot spread
2 tablespoons unsweetened orange juice
2 tablespoons spicy hot mustard
1 teaspoon low-sodium soy sauce
½ teaspoon peeled, grated gingerroot

Arrange ham slices in a 13- x 9- x 2-inch baking dish coated with cooking spray. Combine apricot spread and remaining ingredients; spoon mixture evenly over ham slices.

Cover and bake at 325° for 15 minutes or until thoroughly heated. Yield: 8 servings.

Per Serving: 158 Calories (27% from Fat)
Fat 4.7g (Saturated Fat 1.4g)
Protein 19.0g Carbohydrate 10.5g
Cholesterol 48mg Sodium 1198mg

Jamaican Pork Tenderloin

1 (1-pound) lean pork tenderloin
3 tablespoons fresh lime juice
1 tablespoon bottled chopped jalapeño peppers
1 teaspoon bottled minced fresh garlic
1 teaspoon bottled minced fresh gingerroot
¼ teaspoon salt
¼ teaspoon ground allspice
Vegetable cooking spray
¼ cup mango chutney

Trim fat from pork. Combine lime juice and next 5 ingredients in a large heavy-duty, zip-top plastic bag. Add pork; seal bag, and marinate in refrigerator 30 minutes. Remove pork from bag, reserving marinade.

Coat grill rack with cooking spray; place on grill over medium coals (300° to 350°). Place pork on rack, and grill, covered, 30 minutes or until meat thermometer registers 160°, turning and basting pork occasionally. Cut into ¼-inch-thick slices. Serve with chutney. Yield: 4 servings.

Per Serving: 198 Calories (20% from Fat)
Fat 4.5g (Saturated Fat 1.5g)
Protein 26.2g Carbohydrate 12.4g
Cholesterol 83mg Sodium 241mg

HOISIN PORK MEDAILLONS

(pictured on page 58)

Vegetable cooking spray
1 teaspoon dark sesame oil
1/8 teaspoon dried crushed red pepper
1 clove garlic, minced
1 (1-pound) pork tenderloin, cut into 1/2-inch-thick slices
2 tablespoons water
2 tablespoons dry sherry
1 tablespoon hoisin sauce
1 teaspoon dried cilantro
2 cups cooked long-grain rice (cooked without salt or fat)
1/4 cup sliced green onions

Coat a nonstick skillet with cooking spray; add oil. Place skillet over medium-high heat until hot. Add red pepper and garlic; sauté 1 minute. Add pork, and cook 4 to 5 minutes on each side or until browned. Transfer to a serving platter, and keep warm. Wipe pan drippings from skillet.

Add water and next 3 ingredients to skillet; stir well. Cook over medium heat 1 minute or until slightly thickened, stirring constantly.

Serve medaillons over rice; top with sauce, and sprinkle with green onions. Yield: 4 servings.

PER SERVING: 281 CALORIES (18% FROM FAT)
FAT 5.7G (SATURATED FAT 1.7G)
PROTEIN 28.1G CARBOHYDRATE 26.9G
CHOLESTEROL 83MG SODIUM 166MG

Handy Substitutions

Oriental ingredients, such as sesame oil and hoisin sauce (a thick, sweet, spicy sauce), are available in most supermarkets. A simple substitute for hoisin sauce is equal parts of brown sugar and reduced-sodium soy sauce with a dash of garlic powder.

PEACHY PORK MEDAILLONS

2 (3/4-pound) pork tenderloins
Vegetable cooking spray
1/2 cup peach nectar
1/4 cup Chablis or other dry white wine
1 teaspoon peeled, minced gingerroot
1/4 teaspoon pepper
1 teaspoon cornstarch
1 tablespoon water
1/3 cup mango chutney
2 cups peeled, sliced fresh peaches
1/2 cup sliced green onions
Green onion curls (optional)

Partially freeze tenderloins; trim fat from tenderloins. Cut tenderloins diagonally across grain into 1/4-inch-thick slices.

Coat a large nonstick skillet with cooking spray. Place over medium-high heat until hot. Add half of pork, and cook 3 minutes on each side or until pork is lightly browned. Remove pork from skillet. Drain; set aside, and keep warm. Repeat procedure with remaining pork slices. Wipe drippings from skillet with a paper towel. Combine peach nectar and next 3 ingredients in skillet. Return pork to skillet. Bring to a boil; cover, reduce heat, and simmer 4 to 5 minutes or until pork is tender.

Transfer pork to a serving platter, using a slotted spoon. Set aside, and keep warm. Combine cornstarch and water; stir until smooth. Add cornstarch mixture and chutney to peach nectar mixture; stir well. Add peaches and sliced green onions. Bring to a boil; reduce heat, and simmer, stirring constantly, until thickened. Spoon peach mixture over pork. Garnish with green onion curls, if desired. Yield: 6 servings.

PER SERVING: 231 CALORIES (18% FROM FAT)
FAT 4.6G (SATURATED FAT 1.5G)
PROTEIN 26.7G CARBOHYDRATE 20.7G
CHOLESTEROL 83MG SODIUM 94MG

Peachy Pork Medaillons

Minted Lamb Chops

Minted Lamb Chops

4 (4-ounce) lean lamb loin chops
½ cup Burgundy or other dry red wine
1 teaspoon dried rosemary, crushed
1 teaspoon dried mint flakes
½ teaspoon bottled minced fresh garlic
¼ teaspoon salt
Vegetable cooking spray
¼ cup mint jelly

Trim fat from chops. Combine chops and next 4 ingredients in a large heavy-duty, zip-top plastic bag. Seal bag; marinate in refrigerator 8 hours, turning bag occasionally.

Remove chops from bag, reserving marinade. Sprinkle chops with salt. Coat grill rack with cooking spray; place on grill over medium-hot coals (350° to 400°). Place chops on rack; grill, covered, 6 minutes on each side or until done, basting occasionally with reserved marinade.

Serve 1 tablespoon mint jelly with each chop. Yield: 2 servings.

PER SERVING: 363 CALORIES (25% FROM FAT)
FAT 10.2G (SATURATED FAT 3.5G)
PROTEIN 30.2G CARBOHYDRATE 28.2G
CHOLESTEROL 95MG SODIUM 405MG

Tangy Lamb Chops Veronique

½ cup fine, dry breadcrumbs
2 teaspoons dried dillweed
½ teaspoon garlic powder
¼ teaspoon pepper
8 (3-ounce) lean lamb loin chops (¾ inch thick)
3 tablespoons hot-sweet mustard
3 tablespoons cider vinegar
Vegetable cooking spray
½ cup seedless green grapes, quartered
½ cup seedless red grapes, quartered

Combine first 4 ingredients in a shallow bowl; stir well, and set aside.

Trim fat from lamb chops. Combine mustard and vinegar; brush mustard mixture evenly over chops. Dredge chops in breadcrumb mixture.

Coat a large nonstick skillet with cooking spray; place over medium heat until hot. Add chops; cover and cook 4 minutes on each side or until browned. Uncover and cook 5 minutes on each side or to desired degree of doneness. Transfer chops to a serving platter, and sprinkle evenly with grapes. Yield: 4 servings.

PER SERVING: 254 CALORIES (30% FROM FAT)
FAT 8.4G (SATURATED FAT 2.7G)
PROTEIN 26.4G CARBOHYDRATE 17.5G
CHOLESTEROL 75MG SODIUM 280MG

Chicken Vermicelli

Vegetable cooking spray
1 pound freshly ground uncooked chicken thighs
2 cups sliced fresh mushrooms
1 cup chopped onion
1 teaspoon dried Italian seasoning
1 teaspoon coarsely ground pepper
¼ teaspoon garlic powder
1 (25½-ounce) jar commercial nonfat chunky Italian-style vegetable pasta sauce
5 cups cooked vermicelli (cooked without salt or fat)

Coat a large nonstick skillet with cooking spray, and place over medium-high heat until hot. Add chicken, mushrooms, and onion; cook until chicken is browned, stirring until it crumbles. Drain well, and wipe drippings from skillet with a paper towel.

Return chicken mixture to skillet; stir in Italian seasoning and next 3 ingredients. Cover and cook over medium heat 8 minutes or until thoroughly heated. Serve 1 cup chicken mixture over 1 cup vermicelli. Yield: 5 servings.

PER SERVING: 373 CALORIES (18% FROM FAT)
FAT 7.6G (SATURATED FAT 2.0G)
PROTEIN 26.4G CARBOHYDRATE 48.2G
CHOLESTEROL 63MG SODIUM 517MG

Citrus-Ginger Chicken

Citrus-Ginger Chicken

¼ cup low-sugar orange marmalade
1 tablespoon honey mustard
¾ teaspoon ground ginger
⅛ teaspoon ground red pepper
4 (4-ounce) skinned, boned chicken breast halves
Vegetable cooking spray
2 cups cooked couscous (cooked without salt or fat)
Orange Sauce
Orange zest (optional)

Combine first 4 ingredients in a small bowl, stirring with a wire whisk to blend. Brush half of mixture over chicken. Reserve remaining half.

Coat a grill rack with cooking spray; place on grill over medium-hot coals (350° to 400°). Place chicken on rack; grill, covered, 8 to 10 minutes on each side or until chicken is done, basting occasionally with reserved marmalade mixture.

Place couscous on a serving platter. Arrange chicken over couscous; drizzle Orange Sauce over chicken. Sprinkle with orange zest, if desired. Yield: 4 servings.

Orange Sauce

¼ cup reduced-calorie margarine, melted
½ teaspoon grated orange rind
¼ teaspoon ground ginger

Combine all ingredients; stir. Yield: ¼ cup.

Per Serving: 298 Calories (27% from Fat)
Fat 8.9g (Saturated Fat 1.4g)
Protein 29.9g Carbohydrate 24.1g
Cholesterol 66mg Sodium 224mg

Chicken au Poivre

Flattening the chicken breasts tenderizes them and shortens their cooking time. This recipe goes from cooktop to table in about 15 minutes.

4 (4-ounce) skinned, boned chicken breast halves
2 teaspoons assorted whole peppercorns, coarsely crushed
1 tablespoon reduced-calorie margarine
¼ cup canned no-salt-added chicken broth, undiluted
¼ cup Madeira
¼ cup low-fat sour cream
2 teaspoons all-purpose flour
Assorted whole peppercorns (optional)

Place chicken between 2 sheets of heavy-duty plastic wrap, and flatten to ¼-inch thickness, using a meat mallet or rolling pin. Sprinkle crushed peppercorns evenly on both sides of each chicken breast half, pressing pepper into chicken.

Melt margarine in a large nonstick skillet over medium-high heat; add chicken, and sauté 2 to 3 minutes on each side or until done. Transfer chicken to a serving platter, and keep warm.

Add chicken broth and Madeira to skillet. Bring to a boil; reduce heat, and simmer, uncovered, 2 to 3 minutes or until reduced to ¼ cup. Remove from heat. Combine sour cream and flour; add to broth mixture, stirring constantly. Spoon over chicken. Garnish with assorted whole peppercorns, if desired. Yield: 4 servings.

Per Serving: 174 Calories (26% from Fat)
Fat 5.1g (Saturated Fat 1.8g)
Protein 27.0g Carbohydrate 3.5g
Cholesterol 71mg Sodium 110mg

Microwave Magic

To speed up your grilling, microwave chicken or meat until partially done; then finish cooking it on the grill. (Discard the juices that bleed out of the microwaved meat or chicken.)

Turkey Scaloppine

4 (4-ounce) turkey breast cutlets
1/4 teaspoon freshly ground pepper
3 tablespoons freshly grated Parmesan cheese
3 tablespoons Italian-seasoned breadcrumbs
Vegetable cooking spray
1 1/2 teaspoons olive oil
1/4 cup Chablis or other dry white wine
2 tablespoons fresh lemon juice
2 tablespoons chopped fresh parsley

Place cutlets between 2 sheets of heavy-duty plastic wrap; flatten to 1/8-inch thickness, using a meat mallet or rolling pin. Combine pepper, Parmesan cheese, and breadcrumbs; dredge cutlets in breadcrumb mixture.

Coat a nonstick skillet with cooking spray; add olive oil. Place over medium-high heat until hot. Add cutlets; cook 2 minutes on each side or until browned.

Add wine and lemon juice; cook 2 minutes or until heated. Transfer to a serving platter; sprinkle with parsley. Yield: 4 servings.

Per Serving: 178 Calories (25% from Fat)
Fat 5.0g (Saturated Fat 1.7g)
Protein 29.0g Carbohydrate 2.6g
Cholesterol 72mg Sodium 214mg

Glazed Turkey Kabobs

1 (15 1/4-ounce) can pineapple chunks in juice, undrained
1 pound boneless turkey breast, skinned and cut into 1-inch pieces
2 medium-size green peppers, seeded and cut into 1-inch pieces
1 (8-ounce) can jellied cranberry sauce
2 teaspoons prepared horseradish
Vegetable cooking spray

Drain pineapple, reserving 1/4 cup juice. Thread pineapple, turkey, and green pepper evenly onto 8 (10-inch) skewers; set aside.

Combine cranberry sauce and horseradish in a small saucepan. Add reserved 1/4 cup pineapple juice, and cook over low heat, stirring constantly, until smooth.

Coat grill rack with cooking spray; place on grill over medium-hot coals (350° to 400°). Place kabobs on rack; grill, covered, 12 to 15 minutes or until turkey is done, turning and basting frequently with warm cranberry mixture. Yield: 4 servings.

Per Serving: 283 Calories (14% from Fat)
Fat 4.4g (Saturated Fat 0.9g)
Protein 26.1g Carbohydrate 34.3g
Cholesterol 59mg Sodium 85mg

Southwestern Turkey

Skinned, boned chicken breasts are a good substitute for turkey cutlets.

Vegetable cooking spray
1 pound (1/4-inch-thick) turkey breast cutlets, cut into 2 1/2- x 1/2-inch strips
1 1/4 teaspoons chili powder
1/4 teaspoon ground cumin
1 teaspoon vegetable oil
1 1/4 cups green pepper strips
1 cup thinly sliced onion, separated into rings
1 cup frozen whole kernel corn
3/4 cup commercial thick and chunky salsa

Coat a large nonstick skillet with cooking spray, and place over high heat until hot. Add turkey; stir-fry 3 minutes. Stir in chili powder and cumin. Remove turkey from skillet; set aside.

Add oil to skillet, and heat over medium-high heat. Add green pepper strips and onion; stir-fry 3 minutes.

Return turkey to skillet, and stir in corn and salsa. Stir-fry 2 minutes or until thoroughly heated. Yield: 4 (1-cup) servings.

Per Serving: 211 Calories (16% from Fat)
Fat 3.8g (Saturated Fat 0.9g)
Protein 29.1g Carbohydrate 15.6g
Cholesterol 68mg Sodium 372mg

Southwestern Turkey

Asian-Style Halibut

Poached Grouper

3 (8-ounce) grouper fillets, halved
1 teaspoon dried tarragon, crumbled
¼ teaspoon freshly ground pepper
⅛ teaspoon salt
4 cups water
1 teaspoon olive oil
½ teaspoon minced garlic
¼ cup Madeira
2 tablespoons fresh lemon juice
¼ cup capers
2 tablespoons minced fresh parsley

Sprinkle fillets with tarragon, pepper, and salt. Bring 4 cups water to a boil in a large nonstick skillet over medium heat. Reduce heat, and add fillets; cover and simmer 8 to 10 minutes or until fish flakes easily when tested with a fork. Remove fish from liquid, and place on a serving platter; discard liquid. Set fish aside, and keep warm.

Heat olive oil in a nonstick skillet over medium-high heat until hot. Add garlic; sauté 1 minute or until tender. Add Madeira; cook 1 minute or until reduced to 2 tablespoons. Stir in lemon juice and capers; cook until heated. Pour sauce over fish, and sprinkle with parsley. Yield: 6 servings.

Per Serving: 118 Calories (14% from Fat)
Fat 1.9g (Saturated Fat 0.4g)
Protein 22.4g Carbohydrate 1.5g
Cholesterol 42mg Sodium 544mg

Asian-Style Halibut

2 (8-ounce) halibut or other white fish steaks (about 1 inch thick)
2 teaspoons low-sodium soy sauce
½ teaspoon peeled, finely grated gingerroot
2 cups fresh snow pea pods (about ½ pound)
1½ cups thinly sliced fresh shiitake mushroom caps (about ¼ pound)
4 green onions, sliced into ½-inch pieces
2 teaspoons dark sesame oil
1 teaspoon sesame seeds, toasted

Cut each steak into 2 equal portions, and arrange in an 8-inch square baking dish. Top with soy sauce and gingerroot; cover with heavy-duty plastic wrap and vent. Microwave at HIGH 3 to 4 minutes or until fish flakes easily when tested with a fork, rotating dish a half-turn after 1½ minutes.

Combine snow peas and next 3 ingredients in a 2-quart glass measure; toss well. Cover with heavy-duty plastic wrap and vent. Microwave at HIGH 2½ to 3 minutes or until crisp-tender, stirring after 1½ minutes. Serve with steaks; sprinkle with sesame seeds. Yield: 4 servings.

Per Serving: 193 Calories (26% from Fat)
Fat 5.5g (Saturated Fat 0.8g)
Protein 26.6g Carbohydrate 8.1g
Cholesterol 53mg Sodium 133mg

Orange Roughy Pasta

Vegetable cooking spray
1 clove garlic, minced
1 teaspoon cornstarch
¾ teaspoon dried basil
⅛ teaspoon salt
⅛ teaspoon pepper
¾ cup evaporated skimmed milk
2 cups packed finely chopped fresh spinach
1 pound orange roughy fillets, cut into 1-inch pieces
⅓ cup grated Parmesan cheese
4 cups cooked linguine (cooked without salt or fat)

Coat a 2-quart casserole with cooking spray; add garlic. Microwave at HIGH 30 seconds; add cornstarch and next 3 ingredients. Add milk, stirring well. Microwave at HIGH 3 to 4½ minutes or until slightly thickened, stirring every 1½ minutes.

Stir in spinach and fish. Cover and microwave at HIGH 4 minutes or until fish flakes easily when tested with a fork. Let stand, covered, 1 minute. Stir in cheese; serve over pasta. Yield: 4 servings.

Per Serving: 355 Calories (10% from Fat)
Fat 4.1g (Saturated Fat 1.5g)
Protein 30.6g Carbohydrate 47.4g
Cholesterol 30mg Sodium 348mg

Orange Roughy Veracruz

Orange Roughy Veracruz

2 teaspoons olive oil
1 cup sliced onion
2 cloves garlic, minced
1 sweet yellow pepper, cut into rings
1 (14½-ounce) can Mexican-style stewed tomatoes with jalapeño peppers and spices, undrained
4 (4-ounce) orange roughy or other lean white fish fillets
Dash of garlic powder
Dash of ground red pepper

Heat oil in a large nonstick skillet over medium heat. Add onion and garlic; sauté 7 minutes or until tender. Add sweet yellow pepper and tomatoes; cook over medium-high heat 3 minutes. Add fish; sprinkle with garlic powder and red pepper. Cover, reduce heat, and simmer 5 minutes.

Turn fish. Cover and simmer an additional 5 minutes or until fish flakes easily when tested with a fork. Transfer fish to individual serving plates, reserving cooking sauce in skillet. Keep fish warm.

Place skillet with cooking sauce over medium-high heat, and cook 3 minutes or until thickened. Spoon sauce over fish. Yield: 4 servings.

Per Serving: 149 Calories (21% from Fat)
Fat 3.4g (Saturated Fat 0.4g)
Protein 18.3g Carbohydrate 11.0g
Cholesterol 23mg Sodium 335mg

Sole with Oranges and Grapes

4 (4-ounce) sole fillets
Vegetable cooking spray
4 orange slices
½ cup red seedless grapes, halved
¼ cup unsweetened orange juice
1 tablespoon margarine, melted
¼ teaspoon salt
⅛ teaspoon ground cloves

Arrange fillets in an 11- x 7- x 1½-inch baking dish coated with cooking spray. Top fillets with orange slices and grapes. Combine orange juice and remaining ingredients; stir well, and pour over fillets. Cover and bake at 400° for 15 minutes or until fish flakes easily when tested with a fork. Yield: 4 servings.

Per Serving: 157 Calories (25% from Fat)
Fat 4.4g (Saturated Fat 0.9g)
Protein 21.8g Carbohydrate 6.9g
Cholesterol 54mg Sodium 272mg

Oriental Steamed Trout

1 tablespoon Chablis or other dry white wine
1 tablespoon low-sodium soy sauce
½ teaspoon dark sesame oil
⅔ cup minced green onions
1 tablespoon grated orange rind
1 teaspoon peeled, minced gingerroot
4 (4-ounce) trout fillets
1 medium unpeeled cucumber, sliced

Combine wine, soy sauce, and oil; set aside.

Combine green onions, orange rind, and gingerroot. Line a vegetable steamer with aluminum foil. Arrange fish in steamer; top fish with onion mixture. Place steamer over boiling water. Cover and steam 12 minutes or until fish flakes easily when tested with a fork.

Place fish on a serving platter; drizzle with soy sauce mixture. Arrange cucumber slices around fish, and serve immediately. Yield: 4 servings.

Per Serving: 149 Calories (26% from Fat)
Fat 4.3g (Saturated Fat 0.8g)
Protein 23.3g Carbohydrate 3.8g
Cholesterol 62mg Sodium 154mg

Tuna-Noodle Skillet Dinner

Vegetable cooking spray
2 tablespoons minced fresh onion
⅔ cup water
¼ teaspoon curry powder
¼ teaspoon pepper
1 (10¾-ounce) can one-third-less-salt cream of mushroom soup, undiluted
2 cups cooked rotini (corkscrew pasta), cooked without salt or fat
½ cup frozen English peas, thawed
1 (9¼-ounce) can albacore tuna in water, drained
Chopped fresh parsley (optional)

Coat a large nonstick skillet with cooking spray; place over medium heat until hot. Add onion; sauté until tender.

Combine water, curry powder, pepper, and soup in a bowl; stir well, and pour into skillet. Add rotini, peas, and tuna; stir well. Cook, uncovered, over low heat 10 minutes, stirring occasionally. Sprinkle with parsley, if desired. Yield: 4 (1-cup) servings.

Per Serving: 221 Calories (16% from Fat)
Fat 4.0g (Saturated Fat 1.0g)
Protein 20.0g Carbohydrate 25.4g
Cholesterol 18mg Sodium 219mg

Broiled Lobster Tails

Using the best and freshest lobster tails is a must for this simple recipe. Maine lobsters tend to be sweeter and more tender than spiny lobsters.

4 (6- or 7-ounce) lobster tails
Vegetable cooking spray
2 tablespoons finely crushed saltine crackers (about 4 crackers)
2 tablespoons grated Parmesan cheese
1½ teaspoons minced fresh parsley
Dash of paprika
1 tablespoon reduced-calorie margarine, melted
2 tablespoons Chablis or other dry white wine
2 tablespoons lemon juice
1 clove garlic, crushed

Make a lengthwise cut through the top of 1 lobster shell, using kitchen shears, and press shell open. Starting at the cut end of the tail, carefully loosen the lobster meat from the bottom of the shell, keeping meat attached at end of tail; lift meat through top shell opening, and place on top of shell. Repeat procedure with remaining lobster tails. Place lobster tails on a rack coated with cooking spray, and place rack in a shallow roasting pan.

Combine cracker crumbs, Parmesan cheese, parsley, and paprika in a small bowl; stir in melted margarine. Set aside.

Combine wine, lemon juice, and garlic; stir well. Brush lobster with half of wine mixture. Broil 5½ inches from heat (with electric oven door partially opened) 9 minutes or until lobster flesh turns opaque, basting with remaining wine mixture after 5 minutes. Sprinkle crumb mixture evenly over lobster, and broil an additional 30 seconds. Yield: 4 servings.

Per Serving: 147 Calories (23% from Fat)
Fat 3.7g (Saturated Fat 0.9g)
Protein 22.7g Carbohydrate 3.5g
Cholesterol 110mg Sodium 123mg

Lemon-Parsley Broiled Scallops

1 pound fresh sea scallops
2 tablespoons fresh lemon juice
1 tablespoon olive oil
1 tablespoon water
2 teaspoons minced fresh parsley
1 teaspoon grated lemon rind
½ teaspoon freshly ground pepper
2 cloves garlic, minced

Place scallops in a shallow 2½-quart baking dish. Combine lemon juice and remaining ingredients; stir well. Pour over scallops; cover and marinate in refrigerator 10 minutes.

Broil 5½ inches from heat (with electric oven door partially opened) 6 minutes; stir well. Broil an additional 6 minutes or until scallops are done. Yield: 4 servings.

Per Serving: 135 Calories (29% from Fat)
Fat 4.3g (Saturated Fat 0.6g)
Protein 19.2g Carbohydrate 4.1g
Cholesterol 37mg Sodium 183mg

Shrimp Scampi

2 pounds unpeeled large fresh shrimp
Vegetable cooking spray
2 teaspoons olive oil
8 cloves garlic, coarsely chopped
1 teaspoon seeded, minced red chile pepper
1 tablespoon lime juice

Peel and devein shrimp. Coat a large nonstick skillet with cooking spray; add oil and garlic. Place over medium-high heat 1 minute. Add shrimp and pepper; cook 4 minutes, stirring constantly. Add lime juice, and cook an additional 3 minutes or until shrimp turn pink. Yield: 4 servings.

Per Serving: 149 Calories (27% from Fat)
Fat 4.4g (Saturated Fat 0.7g)
Protein 23.3g Carbohydrate 2.8g
Cholesterol 172mg Sodium 170mg

Curried Shrimp and Rice

½ teaspoon vegetable oil
1 pound medium-size fresh peeled, deveined shrimp
1½ teaspoons curry powder
½ cup low-sodium chicken broth, undiluted
1 (16-ounce) bag frozen broccoli, cauliflower, and carrots
¾ cup uncooked instant rice
¼ teaspoon salt

Heat ½ teaspoon oil in a large nonstick skillet over medium-high heat. Add shrimp and curry powder, and stir-fry 3 minutes. Remove shrimp from skillet, and set aside.

Add chicken broth and vegetables to skillet; bring to a boil, and cook 1 minute. Stir in rice and salt; place shrimp on top of rice mixture. Remove from heat, and let stand, covered, 6 minutes or until liquid is absorbed. Yield: 4 (1½-cup) servings.

Per Serving: 233 Calories (12% from Fat)
Fat 3.2g (Saturated Fat 0.5g)
Protein 27.2g Carbohydrate 23.5g
Cholesterol 172mg Sodium 359mg

Curried Shrimp and Rice

Black Bean-and-Rice Burrito

Black Bean-and-Rice Burritos

1 regular-size bag boil-in-bag converted rice (2 cups cooked rice)
1 tablespoon salt-free garlic-and-herb spice blend
¼ teaspoon ground cumin
1 (15-ounce) can black beans, undrained
6 (8-inch) flour tortillas
¾ cup (3 ounces) shredded reduced-fat sharp Cheddar cheese
¼ cup plus 2 tablespoons sliced green onions
¼ cup plus 2 tablespoons commercial salsa
¼ cup plus 2 tablespoons plain low-fat yogurt

Cook rice according to package directions, omitting salt and fat.

Combine spice blend, cumin, and black beans in a medium saucepan; bring to a boil. Reduce heat, and simmer, uncovered, 5 minutes, stirring occasionally. Remove from heat, and stir in rice.

Spoon about ⅓ cup bean mixture down center of each tortilla. Top each with 2 tablespoons cheese, 1 tablespoon green onions, 1 tablespoon salsa, and 1 tablespoon yogurt; roll up. Yield: 6 servings.

Per Serving: 348 Calories (18% from Fat)
Fat 6.8g (Saturated Fat 2.3g)
Protein 15.2g Carbohydrate 56.4g
Cholesterol 10mg Sodium 438mg

Quick Tip

Want a pizza in a hurry? Split a loaf of French bread in half lengthwise and lightly toast. For the sauce, combine an 8-ounce can of no-salt-added tomato sauce, 2 teaspoons dried Italian seasoning, and ⅛ teaspoon salt. Pile on your favorite toppings (Canadian bacon, mushrooms, green pepper, onion, nonfat mozzarella cheese, or Parmesan cheese); then heat the pizza at 450° for 5 to 6 minutes.

Caramelized Onion Pizza

2 tablespoons reduced-calorie margarine
2 cups thinly sliced yellow onion (about 2 medium)
2 tablespoons sugar
1¼ cups lite ricotta cheese
2 teaspoons Italian seasoning, divided
¾ cup (3 ounces) shredded part-skim mozzarella cheese
¼ cup grated Parmesan cheese
⅛ teaspoon pepper
1 (11-ounce) package refrigerated French bread dough
Vegetable cooking spray
1 large unpeeled tomato, seeded and thinly sliced
¼ cup chopped fresh parsley

Melt margarine in a large skillet over medium-high heat. Add sliced onion and sugar; sauté 5 minutes or until onion is deep golden, stirring frequently. Set aside.

Combine ricotta cheese, 1 teaspoon Italian seasoning, and next 3 ingredients in a bowl; stir well. Unroll bread dough, and pat into a 13- x 9- x 2-inch baking pan coated with cooking spray. Spread ricotta cheese mixture evenly over dough; top with tomato. Sprinkle with remaining 1 teaspoon Italian seasoning and parsley. Bake at 450° for 13 minutes. Top with onion mixture, and bake an additional 5 minutes. Yield: 6 servings.

Per Serving: 271 Calories (28% from Fat)
Fat 8.5g (Saturated Fat 3.4g)
Protein 15.7g Carbohydrate 35.1g
Cholesterol 18mg Sodium 512mg

All-Occasion Salads

A bowl of iceberg lettuce tossed with Italian dressing—it's quick but not very interesting.

For salad pick-me-ups, just turn the page. You'll find ingredients from the exotic papaya to the usual assortment of greens in a wide variety of recipes. Some of the salads can be tossed together in mere minutes, and many can be made ahead.

We start out with fruit and vegetable side salads, and then present an array of main-dish selections. Try the Chili Chicken Salad (page 93) for a summer luncheon or as a light supper entrée.

Pears with Blue Cheese Dressing *(recipe on page 82)*

GLAZED WALDORF SALAD

3 tablespoons lemon juice
3 tablespoons low-sugar apple spread
2 cups chopped Red Delicious apple
⅓ cup raisins
⅓ cup chopped celery
3 tablespoons finely chopped dry roasted cashews

Combine lemon juice and apple spread in a small saucepan; bring to a boil, stirring constantly. Remove from heat, and cool completely.

Combine apple and remaining ingredients in a bowl. Pour lemon juice mixture over apple mixture; toss gently to coat. Yield: 5 (½-cup) servings.

PER SERVING: 103 CALORIES (25% FROM FAT)
FAT 2.9G (SATURATED FAT 0.6G)
PROTEIN 1.4G CARBOHYDRATE 20.4G
CHOLESTEROL 0MG SODIUM 45MG

FRESH FRUIT SALAD WITH LIME CREAM

1½ cups peeled, sliced banana (about 2 medium)
3 tablespoons lime juice, divided
2 cups fresh pineapple chunks
2 tablespoons sugar, divided
1 teaspoon grated lime rind, divided
2 kiwifruit, peeled and cut into ½-inch-thick slices
⅓ cup nonfat mayonnaise
⅓ cup nonfat sour cream
⅛ teaspoon ground mace

Combine banana and 1 tablespoon lime juice in a medium bowl; toss gently. Add pineapple, 1 tablespoon sugar, and ½ teaspoon lime rind; toss gently. Cut kiwifruit slices in half. Add to banana mixture; toss gently. Cover and chill up to 8 hours.

Combine mayonnaise and sour cream; add the remaining 2 tablespoons lime juice, 1 tablespoon sugar, ½ teaspoon lime rind, and mace, stirring well. To serve, spoon ½ cup fruit mixture into each of 8 individual serving bowls; top with 1½ tablespoons sour cream mixture. Yield: 8 servings.

PER SERVING: 82 CALORIES (4% FROM FAT)
FAT 0.4G (SATURATED FAT 0.1G)
PROTEIN 1.3G CARBOHYDRATE 19.3G
CHOLESTEROL 0MG SODIUM 135MG

PEARS WITH BLUE CHEESE DRESSING

(pictured on page 80)

½ cup 1% low-fat cottage cheese
3 tablespoons skim milk
1 teaspoon Dijon mustard
½ teaspoon lime juice
¼ cup crumbled blue cheese
4 large fresh ripe pears
1 tablespoon lime juice
Romaine lettuce leaves (optional)
2 tablespoons chopped walnuts

Combine first 4 ingredients in container of an electric blender; cover and process until smooth. Transfer mixture to a bowl; stir in crumbled blue cheese. Cover and chill thoroughly.

Slice each pear in half lengthwise; remove core. Slice each half lengthwise into ¼-inch slices, leaving slices attached ½ inch from stem end. Brush pear slices with 1 tablespoon lime juice.

Arrange romaine lettuce leaves on 8 individual salad plates, if desired. Arrange pear halves over lettuce, letting slices fan out slightly. Spoon dressing evenly over pear halves, and sprinkle evenly with walnuts. Serve immediately. Yield: 8 servings.

PER SERVING: 108 CALORIES (23% FROM FAT)
FAT 2.7G (SATURATED FAT 0.9G)
PROTEIN 3.6G CARBOHYDRATE 19.4G
CHOLESTEROL 3MG SODIUM 128MG

Melon Salad with Orange-Honey Dressing

Melon Salad with Orange-Honey Dressing

½ medium cantaloupe
½ medium honeydew melon
1 cup seedless red grapes, halved
8 Boston lettuce leaves
1 cup vanilla low-fat yogurt
1 tablespoon honey
1 tablespoon frozen orange juice concentrate, thawed and undiluted
Ground nutmeg (optional)

Peel melons; discard seeds and membranes. Cut each melon half lengthwise into 8 slices. Divide melon and grapes evenly among 4 lettuce-lined salad plates. Combine yogurt, honey, and juice concentrate; stir well. Drizzle ¼ cup over each salad; sprinkle with nutmeg, if desired. Yield: 4 servings.

Per Serving: 162 Calories (8% from Fat)
Fat 1.4g (Saturated Fat 0.8g)
Protein 4.6g Carbohydrate 36.0g
Cholesterol 2mg Sodium 58mg

Marinated Orange-Strawberry Salad

2 cups orange sections
1½ cups sliced fresh strawberries
¼ teaspoon ground cinnamon
¼ teaspoon pepper
⅛ teaspoon salt
1 tablespoon honey
1 teaspoon olive oil
3 cups tightly packed torn leaf lettuce
1 tablespoon pine nuts, toasted

Combine first 7 ingredients in a bowl; toss gently. Let stand 30 minutes. Add lettuce and pine nuts, tossing gently to coat. Yield: 4 (1¼-cup) servings.

Per Serving: 111 Calories (30% from Fat)
Fat 3.7g (Saturated Fat 0.5g)
Protein 2.0g Carbohydrate 20.6g
Cholesterol 0mg Sodium 77mg

Fruit Salad with Yogurt Dressing

1 (8-ounce) carton plain nonfat yogurt
1 tablespoon unsweetened orange juice
1 tablespoon honey
2 cups sliced fresh strawberries
2 cups fresh blueberries
½ medium cantaloupe, peeled and cut into 12 slices

Combine first 3 ingredients in a small bowl; stir well with a wire whisk. Arrange strawberries, blueberries, and cantaloupe on individual salad plates. Top with yogurt mixture. Serve immediately. Yield: 6 servings.

Per Serving: 104 Calories (6% from Fat)
Fat 0.7g (Saturated Fat 0.2g)
Protein 3.5g Carbohydrate 23.3g
Cholesterol 1mg Sodium 39mg

Marinated Orange-Strawberry Salad

Honey-Lemon Fruit Salad

1 (20-ounce) can unsweetened pineapple chunks, undrained
1½ cups (¾-inch) chunks unpeeled firm, ripe pear (about 2 large)
1½ cups coarsely chopped orange (about 2 large)
1 tablespoon lemon juice
1 tablespoon honey
2 teaspoons vegetable oil
¼ teaspoon poppy seeds

Drain pineapple, reserving 2 tablespoons juice; reserve remaining juice for other uses.

Combine pineapple, pear, and orange in a bowl; toss gently, and set aside. Combine reserved 2 tablespoons pineapple juice and remaining ingredients in a jar. Cover tightly, and shake vigorously. Pour over pineapple mixture; toss gently. Cover and chill up to 24 hours. Yield: 10 (½-cup) servings.

PER SERVING: 77 CALORIES (13% FROM FAT)
FAT 1.1G (SATURATED FAT 0.2G)
PROTEIN 0.4G CARBOHYDRATE 17.2G
CHOLESTEROL 0MG SODIUM 1MG

Pineapple Slaw

1 (8-ounce) carton pineapple or vanilla low-fat yogurt
3 tablespoons reduced-calorie mayonnaise
½ teaspoon lemon juice
5 cups thinly sliced cabbage
1 (8-ounce) can pineapple tidbits in juice, drained
Fresh pineapple wedges (optional)

Stir yogurt; spoon onto several layers of heavy-duty paper towels, and spread to ½-inch thickness. Cover with paper towels; let stand 5 minutes. Scrape into a bowl, using a rubber spatula; stir in mayonnaise and lemon juice.

Combine sliced cabbage and pineapple tidbits in a bowl; toss well. Add yogurt mixture to cabbage and pineapple, tossing gently to coat. Cover and chill. Garnish with pineapple wedges, if desired. Yield: 4 (1-cup) servings.

PER SERVING: 119 CALORIES (29% FROM FAT)
FAT 3.8G (SATURATED FAT 0.9G)
PROTEIN 3.6G CARBOHYDRATE 19.1G
CHOLESTEROL 6MG SODIUM 130MG

Pineapple-Carrot-Raisin Salad

2 cups coarsely shredded carrot
¼ cup plus 2 tablespoons raisins
1 (8-ounce) can crushed pineapple in juice, drained
¼ cup vanilla low-fat yogurt
2 tablespoons nonfat mayonnaise
1½ teaspoons creamy peanut butter
⅛ teaspoon ground cinnamon

Combine carrot, raisins, and pineapple in a medium bowl; toss well.

Combine yogurt and remaining ingredients in a small bowl; stir well. Add to carrot mixture, stirring well. Cover and chill thoroughly. Yield: 6 (½-cup) servings.

PER SERVING: 85 CALORIES (10% FROM FAT)
FAT 0.9G (SATURATED FAT 0.2G)
PROTEIN 1.7G CARBOHYDRATE 19.1G
CHOLESTEROL 0MG SODIUM 91MG

Did You Know?

Cabbage, broccoli, cauliflower, and brussels sprouts are all members of that famous food family—cruciferous vegetables. Eat these crunchy veggies often; they contain a substance that seems to fight the development of cancer.

Marinated Green Bean Salad

For the best taste, select very young, tender green beans to use in salads.

1 pound fresh green beans
8 cherry tomatoes, halved
¾ teaspoon dill seeds
½ teaspoon sugar
½ teaspoon dried crushed red pepper
¼ teaspoon salt
2 cloves garlic, sliced
⅓ cup water
⅓ cup white wine vinegar

Wash beans; trim ends, and remove strings. Cut beans into 1½-inch pieces; arrange in a vegetable steamer over boiling water. Cover and steam 3 minutes or until crisp-tender. Plunge beans into ice water; drain well. Combine beans and tomatoes in a large dish. Combine dill seeds, sugar, red pepper, and salt; sprinkle over bean mixture. Add garlic; toss gently.

Combine water and vinegar in a small saucepan; bring to a boil. Pour vinegar mixture over bean mixture, and toss gently. Cover and marinate in refrigerator at least 8 hours, stirring occasionally. Serve chilled. Yield: 8 (½-cup) servings.

Per Serving: 25 Calories (7% from Fat)
Fat 0.2g (Saturated Fat 0.0g)
Protein 1.2g Carbohydrate 5.9g
Cholesterol 0mg Sodium 78mg

Harvard Beet Salad

1 (15¼-ounce) can sliced beets, drained
⅓ cup sugar
⅓ cup cider vinegar
2 teaspoons cornstarch
¼ teaspoon salt
1 tablespoon low-sugar orange marmalade
2 medium oranges, peeled and sectioned
Green leaf lettuce (optional)

Place beets in an 8-inch square baking dish.

Combine sugar, vinegar, cornstarch, and salt in a small saucepan. Bring to a boil over medium heat. Stir in marmalade; let cool slightly. Pour over beets; cover and marinate in refrigerator 8 hours, stirring occasionally.

Drain beets, reserving 2 tablespoons marinade. Combine reserved marinade and orange sections; toss gently. Stir in beets. Arrange salad on individual lettuce-lined salad plates, if desired. Serve immediately. Yield: 4 servings.

Per Serving: 131 Calories (1% from Fat)
Fat 0.1g (Saturated Fat 0.0g)
Protein 1.2g Carbohydrate 33.4g
Cholesterol 0mg Sodium 301mg

Dilled Cucumber Salad

Allow plenty of time for this salad to chill so that the flavors of the cucumber, onion, and dressing will blend together.

2 small cucumbers, thinly sliced
1 small onion, thinly sliced and separated into rings
½ cup white wine vinegar
3 tablespoons sugar
2 tablespoons minced fresh dill
¼ teaspoon salt
⅛ teaspoon pepper

Place cucumber and onion in a shallow baking dish. Combine vinegar and remaining ingredients; pour over cucumber mixture. Toss well. Cover and marinate in refrigerator 8 hours, stirring occasionally. Yield: 6 (½-cup) servings.

Per Serving: 41 Calories (2% from Fat)
Fat 0.1g (Saturated Fat 0.0g)
Protein 0.6g Carbohydrate 10.5g
Cholesterol 0mg Sodium 100mg

Mixed Greens with Tangelo Vinaigrette

MIXED GREENS WITH TANGELO VINAIGRETTE

2 teaspoons coarse-grained mustard
2 teaspoons sherry vinegar
1 teaspoon grated tangelo rind
5 tangelos
1 tablespoon honey
1½ cups loosely packed watercress leaves
1½ cups arugula
1 cup thinly sliced Belgian endive
1 pint fresh strawberries, sliced

Combine first 3 ingredients in a jar; set aside.

Peel and section 2 tangelos; set aside. Squeeze juice from remaining 3 tangelos to measure ½ cup juice. Combine juice and honey in a small saucepan, stirring well. Bring juice mixture to a boil; cook, uncovered, until reduced to ⅓ cup, stirring occasionally. Remove from heat, and cool completely. Add juice mixture to mustard mixture in jar; cover tightly, and shake vigorously.

Combine watercress, arugula, and endive in a bowl; add mustard mixture, and toss gently. Place lettuce mixture evenly on chilled individual salad plates; top evenly with tangelo sections and strawberry slices. Yield: 4 servings.

PER SERVING: 115 CALORIES (5% FROM FAT)
FAT 0.7G (SATURATED FAT 0.0G)
PROTEIN 2.5G CARBOHYDRATE 27.0G
CHOLESTEROL 0MG SODIUM 58MG

Romaine, Endive, and Bean Salad

Romaine, Endive, and Bean Salad

¼ cup water
2½ tablespoons red wine vinegar
½ teaspoon dried oregano
¼ teaspoon pepper
1 clove garlic, crushed
1 (16-ounce) can navy beans, drained
6 cups torn romaine lettuce
2 heads Belgian endive, separated into leaves (about ½ pound)
¼ cup freshly grated Parmesan cheese

Combine first 5 ingredients in a bowl; stir with a wire whisk. Add beans; toss well, and set aside.

Arrange 1 cup romaine on each of 6 salad plates. Divide endive evenly among each serving. Mound ¼ cup bean mixture in center of each salad. Sprinkle each salad evenly with cheese. Yield: 6 servings.

Per Serving: 94 Calories (14% from Fat)
Fat 1.5g (Saturated Fat 0.9g)
Protein 6.5g Carbohydrate 14.1g
Cholesterol 3mg Sodium 203mg

Spinach-Apple Salad with Roquefort Cheese

1 (10-ounce) package washed and trimmed fresh spinach
4 cups cubed unpeeled Granny Smith apple
3 tablespoons white wine vinegar, divided
1 cup peeled, cubed ripe papaya
½ cup unsweetened orange juice
2 tablespoons honey
1 teaspoon Dijon mustard
½ cup (2 ounces) crumbled Roquefort cheese

Remove stems from spinach. Tear into bite-size pieces, and place in a large bowl; set aside.

Combine apple and 1 tablespoon vinegar in a bowl. Toss gently; set aside.

Combine remaining 2 tablespoons vinegar, papaya, and next 3 ingredients in a small saucepan; stir well. Bring to a boil; remove from heat, and immediately pour over spinach, tossing to coat. Top with apple mixture and cheese, tossing gently. Serve immediately. Yield: 8 (1¼-cup) servings.

Per Serving: 97 Calories (23% from Fat)
Fat 2.5g (Saturated Fat 1.4g)
Protein 2.9g Carbohydrate 17.3g
Cholesterol 6mg Sodium 176mg

Spinach-Apple Salad with Roquefort Cheese

German Potato Salad

1½ pounds peeled baking potatoes, cut into ¼-inch slices (about 2 large)
1 cup canned no-salt-added beef broth, undiluted
¾ cup chopped green onions
1 tablespoon sugar
⅛ teaspoon salt
⅛ teaspoon pepper
1½ tablespoons all-purpose flour
¼ cup cider vinegar
⅓ cup chopped, cooked turkey bacon (about 4 slices)
1 tablespoon chopped fresh parsley
¼ teaspoon celery seeds

Place potato in a saucepan; cover with water, and bring to a boil. Cover, reduce heat, and simmer 6 minutes or until just tender; drain. Combine beef broth and next 4 ingredients in a saucepan. Bring to a boil; reduce heat, and simmer 5 minutes.

Place flour in a small bowl. Gradually add vinegar, stirring with a wire whisk until blended. Add to broth mixture, stirring well. Bring to a boil; cook 2 minutes, stirring constantly. Combine potato, broth mixture, bacon, parsley, and celery seeds in a bowl; toss to coat. Yield: 4 (1-cup) servings.

PER SERVING: 167 CALORIES (12% FROM FAT)
FAT 2.2G (SATURATED FAT 1.0G)
PROTEIN 5.4G CARBOHYDRATE 35.0G
CHOLESTEROL 10MG SODIUM 284MG

Couscous Salad

1½ cups water
1 cup couscous, uncooked
1 cup coarsely shredded zucchini
½ cup coarsely shredded carrot
¼ cup thinly sliced green onions
2 tablespoons raisins
½ teaspoon chopped fresh rosemary
¼ cup lemon juice
2 tablespoons olive oil
½ teaspoon salt
½ teaspoon freshly ground pepper

Bring water to a boil in a medium saucepan; stir in couscous. Remove from heat, and let stand, covered, 5 minutes; fluff with a fork.

Add zucchini and next 4 ingredients. Combine lemon juice and remaining ingredients; stir with a wire whisk until blended. Add to couscous mixture; toss well. Cover and chill thoroughly. Yield: 10 (½-cup) servings.

PER SERVING: 105 CALORIES (25% FROM FAT)
FAT 2.9G (SATURATED FAT 0.4G)
PROTEIN 2.7G CARBOHYDRATE 17.4G
CHOLESTEROL 0MG SODIUM 122MG

Garden Pasta Salad

6 ounces corkscrew macaroni, uncooked
3 cups peeled, seeded, and coarsely chopped tomato (about 4 medium)
1 cup peeled, seeded, and chopped cucumber (about 1 medium)
¼ cup chopped green pepper
¼ cup chopped fresh parsley
2 tablespoons sliced green onions
⅓ cup commercial oil-free Italian dressing
Dash of hot sauce
¾ cup crumbled feta cheese
Chopped fresh parsley (optional)

Cook pasta according to package directions, omitting salt and fat. Drain; set aside.

Combine tomato, cucumber, green pepper, parsley, and green onions in a large bowl. Combine dressing and hot sauce, stirring well.

Add pasta and dressing mixture to vegetable mixture, and toss gently. Cover and chill at least 30 minutes. Sprinkle cheese evenly over salad just before serving. Garnish with chopped parsley, if desired. Yield: 6 (1-cup) servings.

PER SERVING: 173 CALORIES (20% FROM FAT)
FAT 3.8G (SATURATED FAT 2.2G)
PROTEIN 6.7G CARBOHYDRATE 28.5G
CHOLESTEROL 13MG SODIUM 313MG

Garden Pasta Salad

Chili Chicken Salad

Wild Rice-Ham Salad

1¾ cups cooked wild rice (about ⅔ cup uncooked), cooked without salt or fat
1¼ cups diced lean cooked ham
½ cup minced celery
¼ cup chopped fresh parsley
¼ cup finely chopped purple onion
¼ cup dried apricot halves
1 tablespoon vegetable oil
1 tablespoon sherry vinegar
1 teaspoon Dijon mustard

Combine all ingredients in a bowl; toss well. Serve at room temperature. Yield: 4 (1-cup) servings.

Per Serving: 222 Calories (26% from Fat)
Fat 6.3g (Saturated Fat 1.4g)
Protein 13.5g Carbohydrate 28.1g
Cholesterol 23mg Sodium 595mg

Chili Chicken Salad

½ cup chopped onion
2 tablespoons chili powder
2 teaspoons ground cumin
1 teaspoon water
¼ teaspoon pepper
2 cloves garlic
1 pound skinned, boned chicken breasts
Vegetable cooking spray
¼ cup Dijon mustard
¼ cup fresh lemon juice
2 tablespoons water
1 tablespoon vegetable oil
1 cup frozen whole kernel corn, thawed
½ cup sliced green onions
6 cups tightly packed sliced romaine lettuce

Position knife blade in food processor bowl, and add first 6 ingredients. Process until a paste forms, scraping sides occasionally. Place chicken in a shallow dish; spread onion mixture evenly over both sides of each piece. Cover and chill 20 minutes.

Place chicken on rack of a broiler pan coated with cooking spray. Broil 5½ inches from heat (with electric oven door partially opened) 5 minutes on each side or until done. Cut chicken across grain into thin slices; set aside and chill, if desired.

Combine mustard and next 3 ingredients in a small bowl; stir with a wire whisk until blended. Stir in corn and green onions.

Divide sliced lettuce evenly among 4 salad plates, and top with warm or chilled chicken slices. Pour dressing evenly over salads. Yield: 4 servings.

Per Serving: 273 Calories (30% from Fat)
Fat 9.0g (Saturated Fat 1.7g)
Protein 30.3g Carbohydrate 18.7g
Cholesterol 72mg Sodium 559mg

Tropical Shrimp Salad

(pictured on page 2)

1 pound medium-size fresh shrimp
3 cups water
1 medium banana, cut into ½-inch slices
1 tablespoon lemon juice
½ small fresh pineapple, peeled, cored, and sliced
1 small ripe mango, peeled, seeded, and sliced
1 kiwifruit, peeled and cut into 8 pieces
4 green leaf lettuce leaves
¼ cup unsweetened orange juice
3 tablespoons reduced-calorie mayonnaise
1 tablespoon honey
Dash of ground ginger

Peel and devein shrimp. Bring water to a boil; add shrimp, and cook 3 to 5 minutes or until shrimp turn pink. Drain; rinse with cold water.

Brush banana slices with lemon juice. Arrange shrimp, banana slices, pineapple, mango, and kiwifruit on lettuce-lined plates. Combine orange juice and remaining ingredients in container of an electric blender; cover and process 5 seconds. Drizzle over salads. Yield: 4 servings.

Per Serving: 219 Calories (18% from Fat)
Fat 4.4g (Saturated Fat 0.8g)
Protein 14.8g Carbohydrate 32.3g
Cholesterol 128mg Sodium 230mg

Orange Curry Dressing

Enjoy this sweet, creamy, fat-free dressing with your favorite combination of fresh fruit.

1 (8-ounce) carton plain nonfat yogurt
¼ cup low-sugar orange marmalade
1 teaspoon lemon juice
½ teaspoon curry powder
¼ teaspoon ground ginger

Combine all ingredients in a bowl, stirring well. Cover; chill thoroughly. Serve with fresh fruit. Yield: 1 cup plus 2 tablespoons.

Per Tablespoon: 8 Calories (0% from Fat)
Fat 0.0g (Saturated Fat 0.0g)
Protein 0.8g Carbohydrate 1.2g
Cholesterol 0mg Sodium 10mg

Creamy Blue Cheese Dressing

½ cup plain nonfat yogurt
½ cup nonfat mayonnaise
¼ cup plus 3 tablespoons skim milk
¼ cup crumbled blue cheese
2 tablespoons lemon juice
½ teaspoon minced fresh garlic
⅛ teaspoon freshly ground pepper
Dash of hot sauce

Combine all ingredients in a small bowl, stirring well. Cover and chill. Serve with salad greens. Yield: 1½ cups.

Per Tablespoon: 13 Calories (28% from Fat)
Fat 0.4g (Saturated Fat 0.2g)
Protein 0.7g Carbohydrate 1.7g
Cholesterol 1mg Sodium 86mg

Green Goddess Dressing

A cottage cheese and buttermilk blend is the perfect low-fat substitute for mayonnaise in this classic salad dressing.

½ cup 1% low-fat cottage cheese
¼ cup plus 2 tablespoons nonfat buttermilk
2 tablespoons chopped fresh parsley
⅛ teaspoon salt
1 tablespoon cider vinegar
⅛ teaspoon hot sauce
1 small clove garlic, crushed

Combine all ingredients in container of an electric blender; cover and process until smooth. Serve over salad greens. Yield: 1 cup.

Per Tablespoon: 9 Calories (20% from Fat)
Fat 0.2g (Saturated Fat 0.1g)
Protein 1.1g Carbohydrate 0.6g
Cholesterol 0mg Sodium 51mg

Rosy Italian Dressing

½ cup plus 1 tablespoon nonfat buttermilk
¼ cup plus 1 tablespoon nonfat mayonnaise
¼ cup no-salt-added tomato juice
1 tablespoon grated onion
¼ teaspoon dried oregano
¼ teaspoon dried basil
¼ teaspoon pepper
¼ teaspoon paprika
1 clove garlic, crushed

Combine all ingredients in a small bowl, stirring well with a wire whisk. Cover and chill. Serve with salad greens. Yield: 1 cup plus 2 tablespoons.

Per Tablespoon: 8 Calories (0% from Fat)
Fat 0.0g (Saturated Fat 0.0g)
Protein 0.4g Carbohydrate 1.6g
Cholesterol 0mg Sodium 62mg

Green Goddess Dressing

SIDE SERVINGS

Grandma may have simmered her green beans for hours, but today's cooks don't want to be in the kitchen that long. Recipes like Country Green Beans (page 98) and Vegetable Medley (page 108) keep the flavor but have less fat and shorter cooking times than their traditional counterparts. Bouillon granules and herbs take the place of bacon grease, keeping fat to a minimum. And because the cooking times are shorter, fewer nutrients are lost.

Look to the last few pages of this chapter for starchy side dishes containing pasta, rice, or grits. These are all loaded with complex carbohydrates and are recommended for healthy meal plans.

Italian Broccoli and Tomatoes (recipe on page 102)

Micro-Steamed Asparagus with Hollandaise

1½ pounds fresh asparagus
2 tablespoons water
½ cup Low-Fat Hollandaise Sauce

Snap off tough ends of asparagus. Remove scales with a knife or vegetable peeler, if desired. Place asparagus in an 11- x 7- x 2-inch baking dish with the trimmed ends toward outside of dish. Add 2 tablespoons water; cover with heavy-duty plastic wrap and vent. Microwave at HIGH 7 minutes or until crisp-tender. Let stand, covered, 2 minutes; drain. To serve, spoon 2 tablespoons Low-Fat Hollandaise Sauce over each serving of asparagus. Yield: 4 (1-cup) servings.

Per Serving: 74 Calories (30% from Fat)
Fat 2.5g (Saturated Fat 0.6g)
Protein 5.0g Carbohydrate 10.6g
Cholesterol 1mg Sodium 78mg

Low-Fat Hollandaise Sauce

1½ tablespoons cornstarch
½ teaspoon dry mustard
⅔ cup 1% low-fat milk
2 tablespoons frozen egg substitute, thawed
2½ tablespoons fresh lemon juice
2 teaspoons margarine
⅛ teaspoon salt

Combine cornstarch and mustard in a 2-cup glass measure. Gradually add milk and egg substitute, blending with a wire whisk. Microwave at HIGH 1 minute; stir. Microwave at HIGH an additional 1½ minutes or until thickened, stirring every 30 seconds. Add lemon juice, margarine, and salt; stir with a wire whisk. Serve over asparagus, broccoli, or other vegetables.Yield: 1 cup.

Per Tablespoon: 13 Calories (42% from Fat)
Fat 0.6g (Saturated Fat 0.2g)
Protein 0.6g Carbohydrate 1.4g
Cholesterol 0mg Sodium 32mg

Country Green Beans

1 pound fresh green beans
1¾ cups peeled, seeded, and chopped tomato
⅓ cup canned no-salt-added beef broth
2 ounces reduced-fat, low-salt ham, diced
1 teaspoon minced garlic
2 tablespoons chopped fresh parsley
1 teaspoon dried thyme
¼ teaspoon pepper

Wash beans; trim ends, and remove strings. Arrange beans in a vegetable steamer over boiling water; cover and steam 10 minutes. Set aside.

Combine tomato, broth, ham, and garlic in a large saucepan. Cook, uncovered, over medium heat 3 minutes, stirring frequently. Stir in beans, parsley, thyme, and pepper. Cover; cook over low heat 10 minutes or until beans are tender. Yield: 4 servings.

Per Serving: 74 Calories (13% from Fat)
Fat 1.1g (Saturated Fat 0.3g)
Protein 5.4g Carbohydrate 12.8g
Cholesterol 7mg Sodium 126mg

Calico Lima Beans

Vegetable cooking spray
1 teaspoon reduced-calorie margarine
⅔ cup chopped onion
½ cup chopped celery
½ cup chopped green pepper
1 (16-ounce) package frozen lima beans
1 cup seeded, diced tomato
1 cup spicy-hot vegetable juice cocktail

Coat a large nonstick skillet with cooking spray; add margarine. Place over medium heat until margarine melts. Add onion, celery, and green pepper; sauté until tender. Stir in lima beans, tomato, and vegetable juice cocktail. Bring to a boil; cover, reduce heat, and simmer 12 to 15 minutes or until beans are tender. Yield: 9 (½-cup) servings.

Per Serving: 81 Calories (6% from Fat)
Fat 0.6g (Saturated Fat 0.1g)
Protein 4.3g Carbohydrate 15.1g
Cholesterol 0mg Sodium 185mg

San Antonio Beans

San Antonio Beans

Vegetable cooking spray
½ cup chopped green pepper
¼ cup chopped onion
1 (16-ounce) can pinto beans, drained
1 (15-ounce) can red kidney beans, drained
¾ cup no-salt-added tomato sauce
2 to 3 tablespoons no-salt-added salsa
1 tablespoon prepared mustard
1 teaspoon liquid smoke

Coat a saucepan with cooking spray; place over medium-high heat until hot. Add green pepper and onion; sauté until tender. Add pinto beans and remaining ingredients. Cover, reduce heat, and simmer 10 minutes or until thoroughly heated. Yield: 7 (½-cup) servings.

Per Serving: 108 Calories (7% from Fat)
Fat 0.8g (Saturated Fat 0.1g)
Protein 6.0g Carbohydrate 19.8g
Cholesterol 0mg Sodium 243mg

Caraway Brussels Sprouts and Pearl Onions

½ pound fresh pearl onions, unpeeled (about 1 pint)
1½ pounds fresh brussels sprouts (about 2 pints)
1 cup canned no-salt-added chicken broth
¼ teaspoon sugar
¼ teaspoon dried thyme
1 bay leaf
½ teaspoon caraway seeds
1 tablespoon reduced-calorie margarine

Drop onions into a large pot of boiling water; return to a boil. Drain; rinse with cold water. Drain well; peel and set aside.

Wash brussels sprouts under cold running water, and remove discolored leaves. Cut off stem ends, and slash bottom of each sprout with a shallow "X." Combine onions, brussels sprouts, and next 4 ingredients in a large skillet; bring to a boil. Cover, reduce heat, and simmer 8 minutes or until brussels sprouts are crisp-tender.

Uncover and cook over medium-high heat 5 minutes or until liquid is nearly evaporated, stirring frequently. Discard bay leaf. Stir in caraway seeds; cook 1 minute. Remove from heat; add margarine, tossing well. Serve warm. Yield: 8 (½-cup) servings.

PER SERVING: 54 CALORIES (20% FROM FAT)
FAT 1.2G (SATURATED FAT 0.2G)
PROTEIN 2.9G CARBOHYDRATE 9.8G
CHOLESTEROL 0MG SODIUM 36MG

Caraway Brussels Sprouts and Pearl Onions

Citrus Broccoli

Citrus Broccoli

1½ pounds fresh broccoli
1 tablespoon reduced-calorie margarine
1 tablespoon all-purpose flour
1 teaspoon grated orange rind
¾ cup unsweetened orange juice

Trim off large leaves of broccoli, and remove tough ends of lower stalks. Wash broccoli, and cut into flowerets. Arrange flowerets in a vegetable steamer over boiling water. Cover broccoli, and steam 3 to 5 minutes or until crisp-tender. Transfer broccoli to a serving bowl, and keep warm.

Melt margarine in a small heavy saucepan over medium heat. Add flour, stirring until smooth. Cook 1 minute, stirring constantly. Gradually add orange rind and orange juice; cook, stirring constantly, until mixture is thickened and bubbly. Pour sauce evenly over broccoli. Yield: 6 servings.

PER SERVING: 58 CALORIES (22% FROM FAT)
FAT 1.4G (SATURATED FAT 0.2G)
PROTEIN 3.6G CARBOHYDRATE 10.0G
CHOLESTEROL 0MG SODIUM 44MG

Italian Broccoli and Tomatoes

(pictured on page 96)

1 pound fresh broccoli
2 medium tomatoes, cut into 8 wedges
2 tablespoons water
½ teaspoon garlic powder
½ teaspoon dried oregano
½ cup (2 ounces) shredded nonfat mozzarella cheese
2 tablespoons sliced ripe olives

Trim off large leaves of broccoli, and remove tough ends of lower stalks. Wash broccoli and cut into small spears. Arrange broccoli in a vegetable steamer over boiling water. Cover and steam 5 to 8 minutes or until crisp-tender. Drain; place in saucepan.

Add tomato wedges, water, garlic powder, and oregano to pan; stir gently. Cook, uncovered, over medium-low heat 10 to 15 minutes or until thoroughly heated, stirring occasionally. Sprinkle with cheese and olives. Remove from heat. Cover and let stand 2 to 3 minutes or until cheese melts. Yield: 8 (½-cup) servings.

Per Serving: 37 Calories (22% from Fat)
Fat 0.9g (Saturated Fat 0.2g)
Protein 3.8g Carbohydrate 4.9g
Cholesterol 1mg Sodium 111mg

Apple Sweet-Sour Cabbage

Vegetable cooking spray
½ cup sliced green onions
4 cups shredded red cabbage
2 medium-size Red Delicious apples, sliced
3 tablespoons brown sugar
¼ teaspoon salt
⅛ teaspoon pepper
½ cup unsweetened apple juice
¼ cup plus 2 tablespoons cider vinegar

Coat a large nonstick skillet with cooking spray; place over medium-high heat until hot. Add green onions, and sauté 2 to 3 minutes or until tender. Add shredded red cabbage and remaining ingredients; toss well. Cook, uncovered, over medium heat 15 to 18 minutes or until cabbage is tender, stirring occasionally. Yield: 7 (½-cup) servings.

Per Serving: 65 Calories (6% from Fat)
Fat 0.4g (Saturated Fat 0.1g)
Protein 0.8g Carbohydrate 16.2g
Cholesterol 0mg Sodium 92mg

Orange-Glazed Carrots and Grapes

2 (10-ounce) packages frozen whole baby carrots
2 tablespoons brown sugar
2 teaspoons cornstarch
¼ teaspoon ground ginger
⅛ teaspoon salt
¾ cup unsweetened orange juice
1 cup seedless red grapes, halved

Cook carrots according to package directions, omitting salt; set aside.

Combine brown sugar, cornstarch, ginger, and salt in a saucepan. Gradually add orange juice, stirring with a wire whisk until blended. Bring to a boil over medium heat; cook 1 minute, stirring constantly. Add carrots and grapes; cook 2 minutes or until heated, stirring occasionally. Yield: 4 (1-cup) servings.

Note: 1¼ pounds fresh baby carrots, scraped, may be used instead of frozen. Arrange in a vegetable steamer over boiling water. Cover and steam 10 minutes or until crisp-tender; set aside. Continue as directed.

Per Serving: 127 Calories (4% from Fat)
Fat 0.5g (Saturated Fat 0.1g)
Protein 2.1g Carbohydrate 30.5g
Cholesterol 0mg Sodium 160mg

Orange-Glazed Carrots and Grapes

Oven-Fried Eggplant

½ cup nonfat mayonnaise
1 tablespoon minced onion
12 (½-inch) slices unpeeled eggplant (about 1 pound)
⅓ cup fine, dry breadcrumbs
⅓ cup grated Parmesan cheese
½ teaspoon dried Italian seasoning
Vegetable cooking spray

Combine mayonnaise and minced onion; stir well. Spread evenly over both sides of eggplant slices. Combine breadcrumbs, Parmesan cheese, and Italian seasoning in a shallow bowl; dredge eggplant in breadcrumb mixture.

Place eggplant on a baking sheet coated with cooking spray. Bake at 425° for 12 minutes. Turn eggplant over, and bake 12 minutes or until golden. Yield: 4 servings.

Per Serving: 120 Calories (20% from Fat)
Fat 2.7g (Saturated Fat 1.4g)
Protein 5.1g Carbohydrate 20.0g
Cholesterol 6mg Sodium 569mg

Sherried Mushrooms

Vegetable cooking spray
½ cup sliced green onions
1 pound sliced fresh mushrooms
2 tablespoons dry sherry
1 tablespoon low-sodium Worcestershire sauce
¼ teaspoon freshly ground pepper

Coat a large nonstick skillet with cooking spray; place over medium-high heat until hot. Add green onions; sauté until tender.

Stir in mushrooms and remaining ingredients; cover and cook over low heat 10 minutes or until mushrooms are tender. Yield: 6 (½-cup) servings.

Per Serving: 26 Calories (14% from Fat)
Fat 0.4g (Saturated Fat 0.1g)
Protein 1.8g Carbohydrate 5.0g
Cholesterol 0mg Sodium 15mg

Stewed Okra and Tomatoes

¾ pound fresh okra pods
Vegetable cooking spray
½ cup finely chopped onion
¼ cup finely chopped green pepper
2 cups seeded, coarsely chopped unpeeled tomato (about 3 medium)
1 tablespoon lemon juice
1 teaspoon dried oregano
¼ teaspoon salt
¼ teaspoon hot sauce

Remove tip and stem ends from okra; cut okra into ¼-inch slices, and set aside.

Coat a medium saucepan with cooking spray, and place over medium heat until hot. Add onion and green pepper; cook 2 minutes, stirring constantly. Add okra, tomato, and remaining ingredients. Cover and cook over medium-low heat 15 minutes or until okra is tender, stirring occasionally. Yield: 4 (¾-cup) servings.

Per Serving: 60 Calories (10% from Fat)
Fat 0.7g (Saturated Fat 0.1g)
Protein 2.6g Carbohydrate 12.5g
Cholesterol 0mg Sodium 164mg

Quick Tip

A food processor can save you time and energy. But if yours is stashed somewhere out of sight, it's probably out of mind as well. Keep the appliance on the counter, and you'll use it more often to slice, chop, and shred your way quickly through food preparation.

Stewed Okra and Tomatoes

Sesame Snow Peas and Red Peppers

¾ pound fresh snow pea pods
Vegetable cooking spray
2 large sweet red peppers, cut into thin strips
½ cup chopped onion
1 tablespoon sesame seeds, toasted
½ teaspoon salt-free herb-and-spice blend

Wash snow peas; trim ends, and remove strings. Coat a large nonstick skillet with cooking spray; place over medium-high heat until hot. Add snow peas, sweet red pepper, and onion; sauté until tender. Add sesame seeds and herb-and-spice blend, stirring well. Yield: 6 servings.

Per Serving: 42 Calories (22% from Fat)
Fat 1.0g (Saturated Fat 0.2g)
Protein 2.2g Carbohydrate 6.5g
Cholesterol 0mg Sodium 3mg

Sesame Snow Peas and Red Peppers

Fancy English Peas

2 (10-ounce) packages frozen English peas
Vegetable cooking spray
1 tablespoon reduced-calorie margarine
¾ cup finely chopped onion
¼ cup finely chopped green pepper
2 tablespoons minced fresh parsley
1 (2-ounce) jar diced pimiento, drained
½ teaspoon vinegar
¼ teaspoon salt
⅛ teaspoon ground nutmeg

Cook peas according to package directions, omitting salt; drain well, and set aside.

Coat a nonstick skillet with cooking spray; add margarine. Place over medium-high heat until margarine melts. Add onion and next 3 ingredients; sauté until vegetables are tender.

Stir in peas, vinegar, salt, and nutmeg; cook until thoroughly heated, stirring occasionally. Yield: 7 (½-cup) servings.

PER SERVING: 79 CALORIES (16% FROM FAT)
FAT 1.4G (SATURATED FAT 0.2G)
PROTEIN 4.4G CARBOHYDRATE 13.1G
CHOLESTEROL 0MG SODIUM 171MG

Lighten Up

By now, we all know it's not what's *in* a potato but what's *on* it that gets us into trouble. The innocent spud, which has 220 calories and only 0.2 gram of fat, often takes the rap for its toppings. Just 1 tablespoon of butter or margarine provides 102 calories and 11.5 grams of fat. One tablespoon of reduced-fat margarine provides half the amount of calories and fat, and low-fat sour cream has only 21 calories and 1.8 grams fat for the same amount. To really keep the fat low, try topping that potato with salsa (it's fat-free), nonfat yogurt, nonfat sour cream, or nonfat mozzarella cheese.

Sweet Potato Wedges

1 tablespoon plus 1 teaspoon margarine
1 tablespoon plus 1 teaspoon unsweetened orange juice
¼ teaspoon ground cinnamon
2 medium sweet potatoes (about 1 pound), peeled and each cut lengthwise into 8 wedges

Place margarine in an 8-inch square baking dish; microwave at HIGH 30 seconds or until melted. Stir in orange juice and cinnamon; add potato, tossing to coat. Cover with wax paper. Microwave at HIGH 6 to 8 minutes or until tender, stirring after 3 minutes. Yield: 4 servings.

PER SERVING: 122 CALORIES (30% FROM FAT)
FAT 4.0G (SATURATED FAT 0.8G)
PROTEIN 1.4G CARBOHYDRATE 20.5G
CHOLESTEROL 0MG SODIUM 55MG

American Fries

3 medium baking potatoes (about 1½ pounds)
½ teaspoon onion powder
½ teaspoon paprika
¼ teaspoon garlic powder
¼ teaspoon salt
¼ teaspoon pepper
Vegetable cooking spray

Scrub potatoes; cut into ¼-inch-thick slices. Pat slices dry with paper towels. Combine onion powder and next 4 ingredients in a large zip-top plastic bag; add potato slices, and shake well to coat.

Arrange potato slices in a single layer on a large baking sheet coated with cooking spray. Bake at 425° for 25 to 30 minutes or until lightly browned, turning after 15 minutes. Yield: 6 (½-cup) servings.

PER SERVING: 85 CALORIES (2% FROM FAT)
FAT 0.2G (SATURATED FAT 0.1G)
PROTEIN 2.5G CARBOHYDRATE 18.8G
CHOLESTEROL 0MG SODIUM 106MG

Glazed Acorn Squash

1 medium acorn squash (about 1½ pounds)
2 tablespoons frozen apple juice concentrate, thawed and undiluted
⅛ teaspoon ground ginger

Pierce whole squash with a fork several times, and place on a paper towel in oven. Microwave at HIGH 4 minutes. Cut squash into 4 wedges; discard seeds and membrane. Place, cut sides up, in an 11- x 7- x 2-inch baking dish. Pierce flesh several times with a fork; set aside.

Combine juice and ginger; stir well, and brush over squash. Cover with heavy-duty plastic wrap; microwave at HIGH 6 to 8 minutes or until tender, rotating dish a half-turn after 3 minutes. Spoon remaining sauce over squash. Yield: 4 servings.

Per Serving: 63 Calories (3% from Fat)
Fat 0.2g (Saturated Fat 0.0g)
Protein 1.0g Carbohydrate 16.2g
Cholesterol 0mg Sodium 6mg

Pattypan Squash with Corn

2 teaspoons margarine
1 small clove garlic, minced
1 cup fresh or frozen whole kernel corn
3 cups cubed unpeeled pattypan squash
2 tablespoons water
1 tablespoon fresh lime juice
¼ teaspoon salt
Dash of pepper

Melt margarine in a large skillet over medium-high heat; add garlic, and sauté 1 minute.

Add corn, and sauté 2 minutes. Add squash and water; cover, reduce heat, and simmer 15 minutes or until tender. Remove from heat; stir in the remaining ingredients. Yield: 4 (¾-cup) servings.

Per Serving: 83 Calories (29% from Fat)
Fat 2.6g (Saturated Fat 0.5g)
Protein 2.6g Carbohydrate 14.9g
Cholesterol 0mg Sodium 178mg

Herbed Tomato Slices

18 tomato slices (½ inch thick)
Vegetable cooking spray
¼ cup plus 2 tablespoons Italian-seasoned breadcrumbs
1½ tablespoons grated Parmesan cheese
2 teaspoons reduced-calorie margarine, melted
1 teaspoon chopped fresh basil

Arrange tomato slices in a 15- x 10- x 1-inch jellyroll pan coated with cooking spray; set aside.

Combine breadcrumbs and remaining ingredients; stir well. Sprinkle breadcrumb mixture over tomato slices. Bake at 350° for 10 to 12 minutes or until thoroughly heated. Yield: 6 servings.

Per Serving: 69 Calories (26% from Fat)
Fat 2.0g (Saturated Fat 0.5g)
Protein 2.7g Carbohydrate 11.5g
Cholesterol 1mg Sodium 248mg

Vegetable Medley

2 cups water
1 teaspoon chicken-flavored bouillon granules
¾ teaspoon dried Italian seasoning
1 clove garlic, minced
2 medium zucchini, cut into very thin strips
2 medium-size yellow squash, cut into very thin strips
2 medium carrots, scraped and cut into very thin strips
1 sweet red pepper, cut into very thin strips
1 tablespoon minced fresh parsley

Combine first 4 ingredients in a large skillet. Bring to a boil; add zucchini, squash, carrot, and sweet red pepper. Cover, reduce heat, and simmer 6 to 8 minutes or until vegetables are tender. Drain well. Transfer mixture to a serving dish, and sprinkle with parsley. Yield: 7 (½-cup) servings.

Per Serving: 26 Calories (14% from Fat)
Fat 0.4g (Saturated Fat 0.1g)
Protein 1.2g Carbohydrate 5.4g
Cholesterol 0mg Sodium 126mg

Vegetable Medley

Cracked Pepper Linguine

Cracked Pepper Linguine

8 ounces linguine, uncooked
¼ cup minced onion
2 cloves garlic, minced
1 tablespoon reduced-calorie margarine, melted
1 (8-ounce) carton nonfat sour cream
1 tablespoon skim milk
1 tablespoon cracked pepper
2 tablespoons freshly grated Parmesan cheese
1½ tablespoons chopped fresh parsley

Cook linguine according to package directions, omitting salt and fat. Drain. Set aside, and keep warm. Sauté onion and garlic in margarine in a small skillet over medium heat until onion is crisp-tender; set aside.

Combine sour cream, milk, and pepper in a small bowl; stir well. Combine linguine, onion mixture, and sour cream mixture; toss well. Sprinkle with Parmesan cheese and parsley. Serve immediately. Yield: 6 (¾-cup) servings.

Per Serving: 193 Calories (11% from Fat)
Fat 2.4g (Saturated Fat 0.6g)
Protein 8.6g Carbohydrate 32.8g
Cholesterol 1mg Sodium 82mg

Tortellini with Cherry Tomatoes and Corn

1 (9-ounce) package fresh cheese tortellini, uncooked
1 (10-ounce) package frozen whole kernel corn
1 clove garlic, halved
2 cups quartered cherry tomatoes
¼ cup sliced green onions
¼ cup chopped fresh basil
2 tablespoons grated Parmesan cheese
1 teaspoon olive oil
⅛ teaspoon pepper

Cook tortellini in boiling water 3 minutes, omitting salt and fat. Add frozen corn, and cook an additional 3 minutes; drain well.

Rub the inside of a large serving bowl with garlic halves; discard garlic. Add tortellini mixture, tomatoes, and remaining ingredients, tossing gently to coat. Yield: 6 (1-cup) servings.

Per Serving: 207 Calories (21% from Fat)
Fat 4.8g (Saturated Fat 1.5g)
Protein 9.3g Carbohydrate 32.8g
Cholesterol 21mg Sodium 194mg

Vermicelli with Tomato-Basil Sauce

8 ounces vermicelli, uncooked
Vegetable cooking spray
1 medium onion, thinly sliced
2 cloves garlic, minced
5 cups peeled, chopped tomato (about 5 medium tomatoes)
1 (8-ounce) can no-salt-added tomato sauce
¼ cup minced fresh basil
⅛ teaspoon pepper
2 tablespoons grated Parmesan cheese

Cook vermicelli according to package directions, omitting salt and fat. Drain well, and set aside.

Coat a Dutch oven with cooking spray; place over medium heat until hot. Add onion and garlic; sauté 5 minutes or until onion is tender. Stir in tomato, tomato sauce, basil, and pepper.

Bring tomato mixture to a boil; reduce heat, and simmer 15 minutes, stirring occasionally. Add vermicelli; cook, uncovered, until thoroughly heated, stirring occasionally. Transfer mixture to a large platter; sprinkle with Parmesan cheese. Yield: 8 (1-cup) servings.

Per Serving: 155 Calories (8% from Fat)
Fat 1.4g (Saturated Fat 0.4g)
Protein 5.8g Carbohydrate 30.8g
Cholesterol 1mg Sodium 47mg

Minted Couscous with Peas

1¾ cups water
2 teaspoons minced fresh mint
1 teaspoon chicken-flavored bouillon granules
⅛ teaspoon salt
1 cup couscous, uncooked
¾ cup frozen English peas, thawed
Fresh mint sprigs (optional)

Combine first 4 ingredients in a medium saucepan; bring to a boil. Remove from heat. Add couscous and peas; cover and let stand 5 minutes or until couscous is tender and liquid is absorbed.

Fluff couscous with a fork, and transfer to a serving bowl. Garnish with mint sprigs, if desired. Yield: 7 (½-cup) servings.

Per Serving: 113 Calories (2% from Fat)
Fat 0.3g (Saturated Fat 0.1g)
Protein 4.2g Carbohydrate 22.5g
Cholesterol 0mg Sodium 179mg

Bulgur Pilaf

2 cups canned no-salt-added chicken broth, undiluted
1 cup bulgur (cracked wheat), uncooked
¾ cup chopped onion
½ cup sliced green onions
½ cup grated carrot
½ teaspoon salt
¼ teaspoon garlic powder
1 tablespoon chopped fresh parsley

Bring chicken broth to a boil in a medium saucepan; add bulgur. Cover, reduce heat, and simmer 15 minutes. Stir in chopped onion and next 4 ingredients; cover and cook 10 minutes or until bulgur is tender and liquid is absorbed. Stir in parsley. Yield: 7 (½-cup) servings.

Per Serving: 89 Calories (9% from Fat)
Fat 0.9g (Saturated Fat 0.2g)
Protein 3.4g Carbohydrate 17.8g
Cholesterol 0mg Sodium 213mg

Garlic Cheese Grits

4 cups water
½ cup skim milk
1 cup quick-cooking grits, uncooked
1 teaspoon minced garlic
¼ teaspoon salt
2 teaspoons low-sodium Worcestershire sauce
¼ teaspoon hot sauce
1½ cups (6 ounces) shredded reduced-fat Cheddar cheese

Combine water and milk in a medium saucepan; bring to a boil. Stir in grits and next 4 ingredients. Cover, reduce heat, and simmer 10 to 12 minutes or until creamy, stirring occasionally. Stir in cheese. Cook, uncovered, over medium heat, stirring frequently, 12 to 15 minutes or until grits are thickened. Yield: 10 (½-cup) servings.

Per Serving: 111 Calories (27% from Fat)
Fat 3.3g (Saturated Fat 1.9g)
Protein 6.9g Carbohydrate 13.4g
Cholesterol 11mg Sodium 196mg

Broccoli-Rice Timbales

1 (10-ounce) package frozen chopped broccoli
Vegetable cooking spray
½ cup chopped onion
1 clove garlic, minced
2 cups cooked short-grain rice (cooked without salt or fat)
½ teaspoon salt
Pimiento strips (optional)

Cook broccoli according to package directions, omitting salt. Drain well, and set aside.

Coat a large nonstick skillet with cooking spray; place over medium-high heat until hot. Add onion and garlic; sauté until tender. Stir in broccoli, rice, and salt. Cook until mixture is thoroughly heated, stirring frequently.

Pack broccoli mixture evenly into 6 (6-ounce) custard cups coated with cooking spray. Invert onto serving plates; garnish with pimiento, if desired. Serve immediately. Yield: 6 servings.

Per Serving: 94 Calories (5% from Fat)
Fat 0.5g (Saturated Fat 0.1g)
Protein 3.0g Carbohydrate 19.8g
Cholesterol 0mg Sodium 207mg

Menu Helper

Keep a supply of boil-in-bag converted or brown rice on hand. For serving with chicken or fish, add 1 teaspoon chicken-flavored bouillon granules along with the rice bag to the boiling water. When the rice is done, stir in a little sautéed chopped onion and garlic.

Broccoli-Rice Timbales

Speedy Soups & Sandwiches

A bowl of homemade soup and a hearty sandwich can be just what you need in the middle of a busy week. Nothing fancy—just simple, satisfying food.

Easier than most soups, each of these can be started in just a few minutes. While the soup simmers, you can make a sandwich, toss a salad, or warm up some bread. To cut down on extra shopping trips, stock your pantry with basic soup-making staples such as reduced-sodium canned broth, evaporated skimmed milk, dry pasta, and canned vegetables.

To perk up a simple turkey sandwich, try different breads and mustards. For a more interesting taste combination, make Open-Faced Beef Sandwiches (page 122). The applesauce in the sour cream topping adds a fruit flavor to the beef.

Cheesy Potato Chowder (recipe on page 120)

Chilled Asparagus-Leek Soup

1 cup chopped leek
Vegetable cooking spray
2 cups (1-inch) sliced fresh asparagus (about 1 pound)
1 (10½-ounce) can low-sodium chicken broth
¼ cup all-purpose flour
½ cup water
½ to 1 teaspoon dried tarragon
1 (12-ounce) can evaporated skimmed milk
¼ cup plain low-fat yogurt
Ground nutmeg (optional)

Place leek in a 2-quart casserole coated with cooking spray; microwave at HIGH 2 minutes. Stir in sliced asparagus and chicken broth. Cover with casserole lid, and microwave at HIGH 10 to 11 minutes or until asparagus is tender.

Place flour in a bowl. Gradually add ½ cup water, stirring with a wire whisk until blended; add to asparagus mixture. Position knife blade in food processor bowl; add asparagus mixture, and process until smooth. Return mixture to dish; stir in tarragon and milk. Microwave, uncovered, at HIGH 6 to 7 minutes, stirring after 3 minutes. Cover and chill. To serve, ladle into bowls, and top with yogurt. Garnish with nutmeg, if desired. Yield: 4 (1-cup) servings.

Note: Soup may also be served hot.

Per Serving: 147 Calories (9% from Fat)
Fat 1.4g (Saturated Fat 0.4g)
Protein 10.7g Carbohydrate 24.1g
Cholesterol 4mg Sodium 138mg

Chilled Asparagus-Leek Soup

Cold Tomato-Yogurt Soup

2 green onions, cut into 2-inch pieces
2¼ cups peeled, chopped round red tomato (about 1 pound)
1 (16-ounce) carton plain low-fat yogurt
1 tablespoon sugar
1 tablespoon minced fresh basil
¼ teaspoon salt
2 drops of hot sauce

Position knife blade in food processor bowl; drop onions through food chute with processor running, and process until finely chopped. Add remaining ingredients; process until smooth. Cover and chill. To serve, ladle into individual soup bowls. Yield: 4 (1-cup) servings.

Per Serving: 110 Calories (17% from Fat)
Fat 2.1g (Saturated Fat 1.2g)
Protein 7.1g Carbohydrate 16.9g
Cholesterol 7mg Sodium 243mg

Basil-Tomato Soup

4 cups peeled, seeded, and chopped tomato
2½ cups no-salt-added tomato juice
1 cup coarsely chopped onion
¼ cup chopped fresh basil
2 cloves garlic, halved
½ teaspoon salt
¼ teaspoon ground white pepper
2 tablespoons reduced-calorie margarine
3 tablespoons all-purpose flour
1½ cups skim milk
Fresh basil sprigs (optional)

Combine first 7 ingredients in container of an electric blender or food processor; cover and process until smooth. Pour tomato mixture into a large saucepan; bring to a boil over medium heat. Cover, reduce heat, and simmer 10 minutes, stirring occasionally.

Melt margarine in a small heavy saucepan over medium heat; add flour, stirring with a wire whisk until smooth. Cook 1 minute, stirring constantly. Gradually add milk; cook over medium heat, stirring constantly, until mixture is thickened and bubbly. Gradually stir sauce mixture into tomato mixture. Cook over medium heat just until thoroughly heated (do not boil).

To serve, ladle soup into individual bowls. Garnish with basil sprigs, if desired. Yield: 6 (1-cup) servings.

Per Serving: 114 Calories (24% from Fat)
Fat 3.1g (Saturated Fat 0.5g)
Protein 5.0g Carbohydrate 19.3g
Cholesterol 1mg Sodium 287mg

Black Bean Soup

1 tablespoon vegetable oil
1 cup chopped onion
2 cloves garlic, minced
2 (15-ounce) cans black beans, drained
½ cup water
1 (14½-ounce) can no-salt-added stewed tomatoes, undrained and chopped
1 (10½-ounce) can low-sodium chicken broth
1 (4-ounce) can chopped green chiles, undrained
1½ teaspoons ground cumin
Dash of ground red pepper
1 tablespoon lemon juice
¼ cup plain low-fat yogurt

Heat oil in a large Dutch oven over medium heat. Add onion and garlic; sauté until tender. Add 1 cup beans; mash with a potato masher. Add remaining beans, water, and next 5 ingredients; stir well. Bring to a boil; cover, reduce heat, and simmer 15 minutes.

Remove from heat; stir in lemon juice. To serve, ladle into individual soup bowls; top each with 1 tablespoon yogurt. Yield: 4 (1½-cup) servings.

Per Serving: 287 Calories (17% from Fat)
Fat 5.4g (Saturated Fat 1.1g)
Protein 15.6g Carbohydrate 47.1g
Cholesterol 1mg Sodium 460mg

Cream of Carrot Soup

Cream of Carrot Soup

Vegetable cooking spray
1 tablespoon reduced-calorie margarine
2 pounds carrots, scraped and thinly sliced
1¼ cups chopped onion
1 cup sliced celery
3 cups canned low-sodium chicken broth, undiluted
1 cup 1% low-fat milk
¼ teaspoon salt
Fresh chives (optional)

Coat a Dutch oven with cooking spray; add margarine. Place over medium-high heat until margarine melts. Add carrot, onion, and celery; sauté 10 minutes. Add chicken broth; bring to a boil. Cover, reduce heat, and simmer 20 minutes. Remove from heat, and let cool 10 minutes.

Transfer mixture in batches to container of an electric blender or food processor; cover and process until smooth. Return puree to pan. Stir in milk and salt. Cook over medium heat just until thoroughly heated (do not boil). To serve, ladle into individual bowls. Garnish with fresh chives, if desired. Yield: 7 (1-cup) servings.

Per Serving: 94 Calories (17% from Fat)
Fat 1.8g (Saturated Fat 0.4g)
Protein 2.9g Carbohydrate 16.6g
Cholesterol 1mg Sodium 173mg

Mushroom and Rice Soup

Vegetable cooking spray
2 tablespoons reduced-calorie margarine
3 cups finely chopped celery
1 cup chopped onion
½ pound fresh mushrooms, sliced
2½ tablespoons all-purpose flour
3½ cups skim milk, divided
¾ teaspoon salt
⅛ teaspoon ground white pepper
1½ cups cooked long-grain rice (cooked without salt or fat)
Fresh celery leaves (optional)

Coat a Dutch oven with cooking spray; add margarine. Place over medium heat until margarine melts. Add celery, onion, and mushrooms; sauté until tender.

Combine flour and ½ cup milk, stirring until smooth; add to vegetable mixture. Add remaining 3 cups milk, salt, and pepper; cook, stirring constantly, until mixture is thickened. Stir in rice; reduce heat to low, and simmer 15 minutes.

To serve, ladle into bowls. Garnish with celery leaves, if desired. Yield: 8 (1-cup) servings.

Per Serving: 124 Calories (17% from Fat)
Fat 2.3g (Saturated Fat 0.4g)
Protein 5.8g Carbohydrate 20.6g
Cholesterol 2mg Sodium 345mg

Creamy Chicken and Mushroom Soup

Vegetable cooking spray
1 tablespoon reduced-calorie margarine
1 cup sliced fresh mushrooms
½ cup sliced green onions
1½ tablespoons all-purpose flour
1 cup skim milk
3 tablespoons water
1 teaspoon chicken-flavored bouillon granules
¾ cup diced, cooked chicken breast

Coat a large saucepan with cooking spray; add margarine. Place over medium-high heat until margarine melts. Add mushrooms and green onions; sauté until tender.

Add flour; cook 1 minute, stirring constantly. Gradually add milk, water, and bouillon granules; cook over medium heat, stirring constantly, until mixture is thickened. Stir in chicken; cook until thoroughly heated. Yield: 2 (1-cup) servings.

Per Serving: 234 Calories (29% from Fat)
Fat 7.5g (Saturated Fat 1.5g)
Protein 27.8g Carbohydrate 14.2g
Cholesterol 61mg Sodium 585mg

Winter Squash and White Bean Soup

1 cup chopped onion
1 tablespoon olive oil
½ teaspoon ground cumin
¼ teaspoon salt
¼ teaspoon ground cinnamon
1 clove garlic, minced
3 cups (¾-inch) peeled, cubed butternut squash (about 1 pound)
1½ cups no-salt-added chicken broth, undiluted
1 (19-ounce) can cannellini beans, drained
1 (14½-ounce) can no-salt-added whole tomatoes, undrained and chopped
1 tablespoon chopped fresh cilantro

Combine first 6 ingredients in a 2½-quart casserole. Cover with casserole lid; microwave at HIGH 3 minutes. Add squash and broth; cover and microwave at HIGH 10 minutes or until tender, stirring after 5 minutes. Add beans and tomatoes; cover and microwave at HIGH 2 minutes or until heated. Stir in cilantro. Yield: 7 (1-cup) servings.

Per Serving: 128 Calories (18% from Fat)
Fat 2.6g (Saturated Fat 0.4g)
Protein 5.7g Carbohydrate 22.1g
Cholesterol 0mg Sodium 210mg

Italian Sausage-Vegetable Soup

6 ounces Italian-flavored turkey sausage
½ teaspoon salt
½ teaspoon garlic powder
2 (14½-ounce) cans no-salt-added stewed tomatoes, undrained
1 (13¾-ounce) can no-salt-added beef broth
1 (10-ounce) package frozen mixed vegetables
¾ cup small seashell macaroni, uncooked

Cook turkey sausage in a large saucepan over medium-high heat until browned, stirring to crumble. Drain; wipe drippings from pan with a paper towel. Return sausage to pan, and add salt and next 4 ingredients; bring to a boil. Cover, reduce heat to medium-low, and cook 5 minutes. Add macaroni; cover and cook 10 minutes or until macaroni is tender. Yield: 7 (1-cup) servings.

Per Serving: 147 Calories (18% from Fat)
Fat 2.9g (Saturated Fat 0.7g)
Protein 8.2g Carbohydrate 21.8g
Cholesterol 15mg Sodium 339mg

Cheesy Potato Chowder

(pictured on page 114)

Vegetable cooking spray
½ cup sliced green onions
½ cup chopped sweet red pepper
1 jalapeño pepper, seeded and diced
3 tablespoons cornstarch
4 cups water, divided
3¾ cups peeled, diced potato
2 teaspoons chicken-flavored bouillon granules
¼ teaspoon salt
⅛ teaspoon ground white pepper
1½ cups frozen whole kernel corn
1 cup (4 ounces) shredded 40% less-fat Cheddar cheese, divided
2 tablespoons minced fresh parsley

Coat a Dutch oven with cooking spray; place over medium-high heat until hot. Add green onions, red pepper, and jalapeño pepper; sauté until tender.

Combine cornstarch and ¼ cup water; stir until smooth. Stir in remaining 3¾ cups water. Add cornstarch mixture to pan. Stir in potato, bouillon granules, salt, and white pepper. Bring to a boil; reduce heat and simmer, uncovered, 10 minutes, stirring constantly. Add corn, and cook an additional 15 minutes, stirring occasionally. Add ¾ cup plus 2 tablespoons cheese; stir until cheese melts. To serve, ladle chowder into individual bowls, and sprinkle evenly with remaining 2 tablespoons cheese and parsley. Yield: 7 (1-cup) servings.

Per Serving: 158 Calories (18% from Fat)
Fat 3.2g (Saturated Fat 1.5g)
Protein 6.0g Carbohydrate 29.7g
Cholesterol 9mg Sodium 438mg

Vegetarian Chili

Vegetable cooking spray
1 cup chopped onion
3 cloves garlic, minced
1 cup water
½ cup diced green pepper
2 tablespoons chili powder
1½ teaspoons ground cumin
2 (14½-ounce) cans no-salt-added stewed tomatoes, undrained
1 (15-ounce) can red kidney beans, drained
1 (15-ounce) can garbanzo beans, drained
¼ cup nonfat sour cream

Coat a Dutch oven with cooking spray; place over medium heat until hot. Add onion and garlic; sauté 5 minutes. Add water and next 6 ingredients; bring to a boil. Reduce heat; simmer, uncovered, 30 minutes. To serve, ladle into individual soup bowls; top each with 1 tablespoon sour cream. Yield: 4 (1½-cup) servings.

Per Serving: 300 Calories (9% from Fat)
Fat 3.1g (Saturated Fat 0.4g)
Protein 16.3g Carbohydrate 55.7g
Cholesterol 0mg Sodium 350mg

Vegetarian Chili

Open-Faced Beef Sandwich

Open-Faced Beef Sandwiches

½ cup nonfat sour cream
¼ cup unsweetened applesauce
2 tablespoons prepared horseradish
½ teaspoon cracked pepper
4 (¾-ounce) slices reduced-calorie whole wheat bread
1 cup shredded fresh spinach
1 cup canned sliced beets, drained
½ pound thinly sliced cooked roast beef
2 tablespoons chopped fresh chives

Combine first 4 ingredients in a small bowl; stir well. Spread 1 tablespoon sour cream mixture over each slice of bread; top each with ¼ cup spinach and ¼ cup beets. Arrange roast beef evenly over beets; spoon sour cream mixture evenly over sandwiches. Sprinkle with chopped chives. Yield: 4 servings.

Per Serving: 175 Calories (30% from Fat)
Fat 5.9g (Saturated Fat 1.8g)
Protein 15.9g Carbohydrate 15.7g
Cholesterol 66mg Sodium 595mg

Turkey Reubens

1½ cups finely shredded cabbage
1½ tablespoons commercial nonfat Thousand Island dressing
1 tablespoon reduced-calorie mayonnaise
1 tablespoon Dijon mustard
12 (1-ounce) slices rye bread
6 ounces thinly sliced cooked turkey or chicken breast
6 (¾-ounce) slices reduced-fat Swiss cheese
Butter-flavored vegetable cooking spray
Cherry tomato halves (optional)

Combine first 3 ingredients in a medium bowl; toss well, and set aside.

Spread mustard evenly over 6 bread slices, and top with turkey. Top each with 1 cheese slice and ¼ cup cabbage mixture. Top with remaining bread slices.

Coat both sides of each sandwich with cooking spray; place on a hot griddle or skillet coated with cooking spray. Cook 2 minutes on each side or until bread is lightly browned and cheese melts. Garnish with cherry tomato halves, if desired. Serve immediately. Yield: 6 servings.

Per Serving: 274 Calories (23% from Fat)
Fat 7.1g (Saturated Fat 2.7g)
Protein 21.0g Carbohydrate 32.4g
Cholesterol 34mg Sodium 497mg

Turkey Reuben

Turkey Rollups

Lower the sodium by using leftover unsalted, roasted turkey instead of turkey from the deli.

¼ cup plus 2 tablespoons (1½ ounces) shredded reduced-fat sharp Cheddar cheese
1 tablespoon thinly sliced green onions
2 teaspoons Dijon mustard
1 (8-ounce) carton nonfat process cream cheese product, softened
6 (8-inch) flour tortillas
12 (1-ounce) slices cooked deli turkey breast
12 large fresh spinach leaves or curly leaf lettuce leaves
24 (⅛-inch-thick) slices unpeeled cucumber

Combine first 4 ingredients in a bowl; stir well. Spread 3 tablespoons cheese mixture over each tortilla. Top with 2 slices turkey, 2 spinach leaves, and 4 cucumber slices; roll up. Yield: 6 servings.

Per Serving: 257 Calories (20% from Fat)
Fat 5.6g (Saturated Fat 1.6g)
Protein 22.1g Carbohydrate 25.6g
Cholesterol 11mg Sodium 983mg

Tomato and Cheese Mini-Pizzas

½ cup commercial no-salt-added spaghetti sauce
4 English muffins, split and toasted
2 tablespoons grated Parmesan cheese
16 (¼-inch-thick) slices ripe plum tomato
4 (½-ounce) slices Canadian bacon, quartered
1 tablespoon minced fresh basil
¼ cup (1 ounce) finely shredded part-skim mozzarella cheese

Spread 1 tablespoon spaghetti sauce over each muffin half; sprinkle evenly with Parmesan cheese. Top evenly with tomato slices and Canadian bacon. Sprinkle muffin halves evenly with basil and mozzarella cheese.

Bake at 400° for 8 minutes or just until cheese melts and pizzas are thoroughly heated. Yield: 8 mini-pizzas.

Per Pizza: 146 Calories (19% from Fat)
Fat 3.1g (Saturated Fat 0.9g)
Protein 6.6g Carbohydrate 23.4g
Cholesterol 7mg Sodium 325mg

Open-Faced Tuna Melt

1 (6½-ounce) can 60%-less-salt white tuna in water, drained
¼ cup chopped celery
1 tablespoon minced sweet pickle
3 tablespoons reduced-calorie mayonnaise
2 English muffins, split and toasted
4 (¼-inch-thick) slices tomato
4 (1-ounce) slices low-fat process American cheese

Combine tuna, celery, pickle, and mayonnaise; stir well. Place muffin halves, cut sides up, on an ungreased baking sheet. Spoon tuna mixture onto each half. Top each with 1 tomato slice and 1 cheese slice. Broil 5½ inches from heat (with electric oven door partially opened) 2 to 3 minutes or until cheese melts. Yield: 4 servings.

Per Serving: 211 Calories (26% from Fat)
Fat 6.0g (Saturated Fat 1.8g)
Protein 18.0g Carbohydrate 20.9g
Cholesterol 13mg Sodium 698mg

Menu Helper

Here are ways to sneak nutrition into your children's diets without a lot of fuss:

- Serve whole-grain breads and cereals.
- Make soft drinks from sparkling water and 100% juice.
- Keep fresh fruit washed and ready to eat.
- Pop your own popcorn, using little fat.

Shrimp Rémoulade Sandwiches

Shrimp Rémoulade Sandwiches

1½ cups coarsely chopped cooked shrimp
⅓ cup chopped celery
3 tablespoons nonfat mayonnaise
1 teaspoon chopped green onions
1 teaspoon capers
½ teaspoon tarragon vinegar
¼ teaspoon salt
¼ teaspoon prepared horseradish
4 (1-ounce) slices oatmeal bread, toasted
1½ cups shredded romaine lettuce
4 lemon twists (optional)

Combine shrimp, celery, mayonnaise, and green onions in a small bowl, stirring well.

Add capers and next 3 ingredients, stirring well to combine. Place bread slices on a serving platter. Divide lettuce evenly among bread slices. Spoon shrimp mixture evenly over lettuce. Garnish with lemon twists, if desired. Yield: 4 servings.

Per Serving: 147 Calories (17% from Fat)
Fat 2.8g (Saturated Fat 0.6g)
Protein 13.5g Carbohydrate 16.3g
Cholesterol 92mg Sodium 550mg

Shrimp Calzones

Shrimp Calzones

1 (10-ounce) package refrigerated pizza crust
⅓ cup Italian-style tomato paste
1 tablespoon water
¼ teaspoon dried Italian seasoning
1 (8-ounce) package frozen cooked salad shrimp, thawed and drained
Butter-flavored vegetable cooking spray
1 tablespoon grated Parmesan cheese

Roll pizza crust into an 18- x 10-inch rectangle. Cut into 6 (6- x 5-inch) rectangles.

Combine tomato paste, water, and Italian seasoning. Spread evenly over rectangles, leaving a ½-inch border.

Arrange shrimp evenly over half of each rectangle. Brush edges of rectangles with water. Fold rectangles in half crosswise over shrimp; press edges together with a fork.

Place calzones on a large baking sheet coated with cooking spray. Coat tops with cooking spray, and sprinkle evenly with Parmesan cheese. Bake at 400° for 18 minutes or until lightly browned. Yield: 6 servings.

PER SERVING: 182 CALORIES (13% FROM FAT)
FAT 2.7G (SATURATED FAT 0.6G)
PROTEIN 12.8G CARBOHYDRATE 24.8G
CHOLESTEROL 74MG SODIUM 370MG

Apple Breakfast Sandwiches

⅓ cup grated apple
½ cup light process cream cheese product
2 tablespoons crunchy peanut butter
1½ tablespoons apple butter
⅛ teaspoon ground cinnamon
12 (1-ounce) slices cinnamon-raisin bread, toasted

Press apple dry between layers of paper towels; set apple aside.

Beat cream cheese in a medium bowl at medium speed of an electric mixer until light and fluffy. Add peanut butter, apple butter, and cinnamon; beat well. Stir in apple.

Spread apple mixture evenly over each of 6 bread slices; top with remaining bread slices. Cut sandwiches in half. Yield: 6 servings.

PER SERVING: 236 CALORIES (28% FROM FAT)
FAT 7.4G (SATURATED FAT 2.7G)
PROTEIN 7.2G CARBOHYDRATE 36.2G
CHOLESTEROL 13MG SODIUM 338MG

Fruit and Cheese Subs

If fresh peaches aren't available, use canned unsweetened peaches. Drain them well before and after chopping.

¾ cup plus 2 tablespoons nonfat herb-and-garlic cream cheese product, divided
1 tablespoon minced fresh dill
1 tablespoon commercial nonfat creamy cucumber dressing
1 cup peeled, finely chopped fresh peaches
1 cup seeded, finely chopped cucumber
3 tablespoons chopped almonds, toasted
1 (16-ounce) loaf Italian bread
6 green leaf lettuce leaves
5 ounces reduced-fat Havarti or Swiss cheese, thinly sliced

Combine ¼ cup cream cheese, dill, and dressing, stirring well. Add peaches, cucumber, and almonds; stir well. Set aside.

Slice bread in half horizontally. Hollow out center of each half, leaving 1-inch-thick shells. Reserve inside of bread for another use.

Spread remaining ½ cup plus 2 tablespoons cream cheese over cut sides of bread. Place lettuce leaves on bottom half of bread. Spoon peach mixture evenly over lettuce. Place cheese slices over peach mixture, and top with remaining bread half. Cut loaf into 8 slices. Yield: 8 servings.

PER SERVING: 229 CALORIES (24% FROM FAT)
FAT 6.0G (SATURATED FAT 2.7G)
PROTEIN 13.0G CARBOHYDRATE 30.7G
CHOLESTEROL 17MG SODIUM 563MG

Fast Finales

Who has time to prepare an old-fashioned dessert? And even if you had the time, could you afford the fat and calories? The truth is desserts don't have to be bad for you to taste good. And, as you'll see in this chapter, they can be quick too.

We've included simple fruit desserts, such as Minty Melon Compote (page 130) and Creamy Fruit Ambrosia (page 132), that are naturally sweet and luscious, as well as cookie and cake recipes, which may use packaged reduced-fat mixes for convenience.

Be sure to try Frozen Raspberry-Brownie Dessert (page 136)—one of the frozen desserts featured in this chapter. Like all make-ahead recipes, it lets you cook on your own schedule. Days or even weeks later, you can immediately satisfy your sweet tooth.

Frozen Yogurt Pie with Raspberry-Graham Crust (recipe on page 136)

Banana Bread Pudding

Our taste-testing panel preferred the microwave version, but you can bake it in the oven at 350° for 45 minutes.

2⁄3 cup evaporated skimmed milk
1⁄2 cup mashed ripe banana
1⁄3 cup frozen egg substitute, thawed
1 tablespoon sugar
1⁄2 teaspoon vanilla extract
1⁄4 teaspoon ground cinnamon
2 (1-ounce) slices French bread, cut into 3⁄4-inch cubes
Vegetable cooking spray
1⁄4 cup reduced-calorie frozen whipped topping, thawed

Combine first 7 ingredients in a bowl; toss gently. Divide mixture evenly between 2 (10-ounce) custard cups coated with cooking spray.

Place cups in an 8-inch square baking dish. Add hot water to dish to a depth of 1 inch; microwave at MEDIUM (50% power) 16 to 18 minutes or until pudding is set. Remove cups from water; let stand 15 minutes. Serve warm or at room temperature with whipped topping. Yield: 2 servings.

Per Serving: 269 Calories (8% from Fat)
Fat 2.4g (Saturated Fat 1.1g)
Protein 13.8g Carbohydrate 47.7g
Cholesterol 4mg Sodium 329mg

Fruited Crème Brûlée

2 cups fresh pineapple chunks
2 cups fresh strawberries, halved
2 medium kiwifruit, peeled and sliced
1⁄4 cup low-fat sour cream
2 ounces Neufchâtel cheese, softened
1⁄3 cup firmly packed brown sugar

Combine pineapple, strawberries, and kiwifruit in a large bowl; stir gently. Spoon fruit evenly into 6 (6-ounce) ovenproof ramekins or custard cups.

Combine sour cream and Neufchâtel cheese, stirring well; spoon evenly over fruit mixture.

Place ramekins on a baking sheet. Sprinkle each evenly with brown sugar. Broil 5½ inches from heat (with electric oven door partially opened) 2 minutes or until sugar melts. Serve immediately. Yield: 6 servings.

Per Serving: 123 Calories (29% from Fat)
Fat 4.0g (Saturated Fat 2.2g)
Protein 2.1g Carbohydrate 21.4g
Cholesterol 11mg Sodium 46mg

Minty Melon Compote

3 cups cantaloupe balls
3 cups watermelon balls
1 cup unsweetened apple juice
2 tablespoons finely chopped fresh mint
1⁄2 teaspoon grated orange rind
4 kiwifruit, peeled and sliced
Fresh mint sprigs (optional)

Combine cantaloupe and watermelon balls in a large bowl. Combine apple juice, chopped mint, and orange rind; stir well. Pour over melon balls; toss gently. Cover and chill 30 minutes. Add kiwifruit, and toss gently. Garnish with mint sprigs, if desired. Yield: 6 (1-cup) servings.

Per Serving: 77 Calories (8% from Fat)
Fat 0.7g (Saturated Fat 0.3g)
Protein 1.4g Carbohydrate 17.5g
Cholesterol 0mg Sodium 8mg

Quick Tip

For an easy dessert, combine ½ cup frozen orange juice concentrate, thawed, with 2 tablespoons honey. Pour the mixture over 4 cups quartered fresh strawberries and toss.

Minty Melon Compote

Creamy Fruit Ambrosia

Creamy Fruit Ambrosia

4 cups cubed fresh pineapple
2 cups peeled, coarsely chopped fresh peaches
1 (8-ounce) carton vanilla low-fat yogurt
¼ cup peach preserves
2 tablespoons shredded coconut, toasted
1 tablespoon finely chopped pecans, toasted

Combine pineapple and peaches in a large bowl; cover and chill. Combine yogurt and preserves; stir well. Spoon 1 cup fruit mixture into each of 6 individual dessert dishes; top each with 2½ tablespoons yogurt mixture, 1 teaspoon coconut, and ½ teaspoon pecans. Yield: 6 servings.

Per Serving: 159 Calories (14% from Fat)
Fat 2.5g (Saturated Fat 1.0g)
Protein 2.9g Carbohydrate 34.6g
Cholesterol 2mg Sodium 36mg

Raspberry Cheesecake Parfaits

If fresh raspberries are not available, use thawed, frozen raspberries or 1 cup sliced fresh strawberries.

¼ cup lite ricotta cheese
¼ cup nonfat process cream cheese product
2 tablespoons sugar
1 cup fresh raspberries
2 tablespoons no-sugar-added seedless raspberry spread, melted
¼ cup plus 2 tablespoons vanilla wafer cookie crumbs (about 10 cookies)
2 tablespoons reduced-calorie frozen whipped topping, thawed

Position knife blade in food processor bowl; add first 3 ingredients. Process until smooth, scraping sides of processor bowl once; set aside.

Combine raspberries and raspberry spread; stir gently. Spoon 1/4 cup raspberry mixture into each of 2 (8-ounce) parfait glasses; top each with 2 tablespoons ricotta mixture.

Sprinkle 3 tablespoons cookie crumbs over ricotta mixture in each glass; top each with 2 tablespoons ricotta mixture. Spoon 1/4 cup raspberry mixture over ricotta mixture in each glass; top each with 1 tablespoon whipped topping. Chill at least 2 hours before serving. Yield: 2 servings.

PER SERVING: 244 CALORIES (22% FROM FAT)
FAT 5.9G (SATURATED FAT 2.1G)
PROTEIN 8.6G CARBOHYDRATE 40.2G
CHOLESTEROL 9MG SODIUM 269MG

ORANGE PARFAITS

2 cups orange sherbet
1/4 cup low-sugar orange marmalade
1 (8-ounce) carton vanilla low-fat yogurt
2 teaspoons grated orange rind

Scoop 1/2 cup orange sherbet into each of 4 parfait glasses; top each with 1 tablespoon marmalade. Spoon yogurt evenly over each; sprinkle 1/2 teaspoon orange rind over each parfait. Serve immediately. Yield: 4 servings.

PER SERVING: 184 CALORIES (13% FROM FAT)
FAT 2.6G (SATURATED FAT 1.6G)
PROTEIN 4.0G CARBOHYDRATE 38.1G
CHOLESTEROL 8MG SODIUM 84MG

Orange Parfaits

Double Chocolate Pudding

Double Chocolate Pudding

¼ cup plus 2 tablespoons sugar
¼ cup unsweetened cocoa
3½ tablespoons cornstarch
3 cups 1% low-fat chocolate milk
1 egg yolk, lightly beaten
1 tablespoon reduced-calorie margarine
¾ teaspoon vanilla extract
1 tablespoon coarsely crushed mint candy pieces

Combine first 3 ingredients in a large heavy saucepan. Gradually add milk, stirring constantly. Cook over medium heat, stirring constantly, until mixture comes to a boil; cook an additional minute.

Gradually stir one-fourth of hot mixture into egg yolk; add to remaining hot mixture. Cook over medium-low heat, stirring constantly, 3 minutes or until mixture thickens. Remove mixture from heat; add margarine and vanilla, stirring until margarine melts.

Pour evenly into 6 (6-ounce) dessert dishes. Cover and chill thoroughly. Before serving, sprinkle pudding with crushed candy. Yield: 6 servings.

Per Serving: 187 Calories (18% from Fat)
Fat 3.8g (Saturated Fat 1.3g)
Protein 5.6g Carbohydrate 33.0g
Cholesterol 40mg Sodium 98mg

Brown Sugar Pudding

Substitute dark brown sugar for sugar; omit unsweetened cocoa. Substitute 2% lowfat milk for chocolate milk; increase vanilla extract to 1 teaspoon. Omit sprinkling with crushed candy. Yield: 6 servings.

Per Serving: 153 Calories (26% from Fat)
Fat 4.4g (Saturated Fat 1.7g)
Protein 4.5g Carbohydrate 23.8g
Cholesterol 46mg Sodium 86mg

Orange Granita

4 cups fresh orange juice
1 cup Basic Sugar Syrup
2 tablespoons orange marmalade

Combine all ingredients in a large bowl, stirring with a wire whisk until blended. Pour mixture into a 13- x 9- x 2-inch baking dish; cover and freeze 8 hours or until firm. Remove from freezer; scrape entire mixture with the tines of a fork until fluffy. Spoon into a container; cover and freeze for up to 1 month. Yield: 14 (½-cup) servings.

Basic Sugar Syrup

2¼ cups sugar
2 cups water

Combine sugar and water in a medium saucepan, and stir well. Bring sugar mixture to a boil, and cook, stirring constantly, 1 minute or until sugar dissolves. Yield: 3 cups.

Per Serving: 80 Calories (1% from Fat)
Fat 0.1g (Saturated Fat 0.0g)
Protein 0.5g Carbohydrate 20.3g
Cholesterol 0mg Sodium 3mg

Raspberry Sorbet

3 cups fresh raspberries
1½ cups Basic Sugar Syrup (see recipe above)

Combine raspberries and 1½ cups Basic Sugar Syrup in container of a food processor; process until smooth. Pour mixture into an 8-inch square baking dish; cover and freeze 8 hours or until firm.

Remove mixture from freezer; break into chunks. Place in container of a food processor; add frozen chunks, and process until smooth. Serve immediately, or spoon mixture into a container; cover and freeze up to 1 month. Yield: 8 (½-cup) servings.

Per Serving: 131 Calories (2% from Fat)
Fat 0.3g (Saturated Fat 0.0g)
Protein 0.4g Carbohydrate 33.4g
Cholesterol 0mg Sodium 0mg

Layered Sherbet Dessert

½ cup vanilla wafer crumbs (about 14 wafers)
½ cup crisp rice cereal
¼ cup reduced-calorie margarine, melted
3 cups raspberry sherbet, softened
3 cups lime sherbet, softened
3 cups orange sherbet, softened

Combine first 3 ingredients; stir well. Firmly press crumb mixture evenly over bottom of a 9-inch springform pan. Bake at 350° for 15 minutes. Remove from oven, and cool completely.

Spread raspberry sherbet evenly over crust; cover and freeze until firm. Repeat procedure with lime sherbet and orange sherbet. Cover and freeze at least 4 hours or until firm.

To serve, remove sides of pan. Slice dessert into wedges. Serve immediately. Yield: 14 servings.

Per Serving: 188 Calories (22% from Fat)
Fat 4.6g (Saturated Fat 1.4g)
Protein 1.5g Carbohydrate 36.5g
Cholesterol 3mg Sodium 133mg

Frozen Yogurt Pie with Raspberry-Graham Crust

(pictured on 128)

¼ cup no-sugar-added seedless raspberry or strawberry spread
1⅔ cups graham cracker crumbs
Vegetable cooking spray
2 cups vanilla low-fat frozen yogurt, softened
2 cups chocolate low-fat frozen yogurt, softened
2 tablespoons semisweet chocolate morsels
2 teaspoons no-sugar-added seedless raspberry spread
1 teaspoon reduced-calorie margarine
Fresh raspberries or strawberries (optional)
Fresh mint sprigs (optional)

Bring ¼ cup raspberry spread to a boil in a small saucepan, stirring with a wire whisk until smooth. Stir in cracker crumbs. Firmly press crumb mixture, using wax paper, evenly into bottom and up sides of a 9-inch pieplate coated with cooking spray.

Spread vanilla yogurt in bottom of pie shell; freeze 30 minutes. Remove from freezer, and top vanilla yogurt with chocolate yogurt. Cover and freeze at least 8 hours.

Heat chocolate morsels, 2 teaspoons raspberry spread, and margarine in a small saucepan over low heat, stirring constantly, until melted. Drizzle chocolate mixture in thin lines over pie. Let pie stand at room temperature 5 minutes before slicing. If desired, garnish with raspberries and mint sprigs. Yield: 8 servings.

Per Serving: 214 Calories (21% from Fat)
Fat 5.1g (Saturated Fat 2.2g)
Protein 3.9g Carbohydrate 40.0g
Cholesterol 9mg Sodium 167mg

Frozen Raspberry-Brownie Dessert

1 (20-ounce) package light fudge brownie mix
Vegetable cooking spray
4 cups raspberry low-fat frozen yogurt, softened
½ cup chocolate graham snacks crumbs (about 44 bear-shaped cookies)
2 cups fresh raspberries or strawberries

Prepare brownie mix according to package directions, using a 13- x 9- x 2-inch baking pan coated with cooking spray. Bake at 350° for 20 minutes. Cool completely.

Spread softened yogurt evenly over cooled brownies. Sprinkle crumbs over yogurt; cover and freeze 5 hours or until firm.

To serve, cut brownies into bars, and top each bar with raspberries. Yield: 16 servings.

Per Serving: 221 Calories (13% from Fat)
Fat 3.1g (Saturated Fat 1.6g)
Protein 3.3g Carbohydrate 44.3g
Cholesterol 5mg Sodium 174mg

Frozen Raspberry-Brownie Dessert

Hawaiian Ice-Box Cake

Hawaiian Ice-Box Cake

This cake tastes best when made ahead of time and served chilled.

1⅓ cups water
3 egg whites
1 (18.5-ounce) package light, 94%-fat-free yellow cake mix
Vegetable cooking spray
2 cups skim milk
1 (3.4-ounce) package instant banana cream pudding and pie filling mix
1 (15-ounce) can unsweetened crushed pineapple, drained
2 cups reduced-calorie frozen whipped topping, thawed
¼ cup shredded coconut, toasted

Combine first 3 ingredients in a large bowl; beat mixture at low speed of an electric mixer 30 seconds. Increase speed to medium, and beat 2 minutes. Pour batter into a 13- x 9- x 2-inch baking pan coated with cooking spray. Bake at 350° for 35 minutes or until cake springs back when touched lightly in center. Let cool in pan on a wire rack.

Combine milk and pudding mix in a medium bowl; beat at low speed of an electric mixer 2 minutes or until thickened. Cover and chill 5 minutes.

Stir pineapple into pudding. Pierce 48 holes in top of cake, using the handle of a wooden spoon. Spread pudding mixture over cake, and then spread whipped topping over pudding mixture. Sprinkle topping with shredded coconut. Store in refrigerator. Yield: 16 servings.

Per Serving: 208 Calories (17% from Fat)
Fat 4.0g (Saturated Fat 1.3g)
Protein 2.8g Carbohydrate 40.4g
Cholesterol 1mg Sodium 341mg

Orange-Blueberry Streusel Cake

¼ cup sugar
2 tablespoons all-purpose flour
2 teaspoons grated orange rind
½ teaspoon ground cinnamon
1 tablespoon margarine
1 (16.5-ounce) package light, 97%-fat-free wild blueberry muffin mix
¾ cup fresh orange juice
1 teaspoon vanilla extract
1 egg white
Vegetable cooking spray

Combine sugar and next 3 ingredients in a bowl; cut in margarine with a pastry blender until mixture resembles coarse meal. Set aside.

Remove blueberries from muffin mix box. Drain and rinse blueberries, and set aside.

Combine muffin mix and next 3 ingredients in a bowl, stirring just until dry ingredients are moistened. Gently fold in blueberries. Pour batter into an 8-inch square baking dish coated with cooking spray. Sprinkle sugar mixture over batter.

Bake at 400° for 25 minutes or until a wooden pick inserted in center comes out clean. Cool in pan on a wire rack. Yield: 9 servings.

Per Serving: 172 Calories (14% from Fat)
Fat 2.7g (Saturated Fat 1.5g)
Protein 2.0g Carbohydrate 36.0g
Cholesterol 0mg Sodium 208mg

Quick Tip

Running short on time and want a dessert that's quick? Skip your recipe file and start with a packaged dessert mix. You can make it healthy by substituting 2 egg whites for each whole egg and equal amounts of skim milk for whole milk, and by using a little less margarine than is recommended on the package.

Thumbprint Cookies

Thumbprint Cookies

1 (17.5-ounce) package regular chocolate chip cookie mix
1 cup regular oats, uncooked
⅓ cup water
1 teaspoon vanilla extract
1 egg white
Vegetable cooking spray
¼ cup plus 2 teaspoons strawberry jam

Combine first 5 ingredients in a bowl; stir well. Drop dough by 2 level teaspoonfuls 1 inch apart onto cookie sheets coated with cooking spray.

Press center of each cookie with thumb, making an indentation; fill with ¼ teaspoon jam. Bake at 375° for 10 minutes or until golden. Yield: 4½ dozen.

Per Cookie: 54 Calories (30% from Fat)
Fat 1.8g (Saturated Fat 1.0g)
Protein 0.6g Carbohydrate 8.8g
Cholesterol 0mg Sodium 28mg

Butterscotch Bars

3 tablespoons margarine
½ cup firmly packed brown sugar
2 cups miniature marshmallows
4 cups oven-toasted rice cereal
2 cups whole wheat flake cereal
Vegetable cooking spray

Melt margarine in a large saucepan over medium heat. Add sugar; stir well. Add marshmallows; cook until marshmallows melt, stirring constantly. Remove from heat; stir in cereals.

Press cereal mixture evenly into the bottom of a 13- x 9- x 2-inch baking pan coated with cooking spray. Let cool for 1 hour. Cut into 3- x 2-inch bars. Yield: 18 bars.

Per Bar: 92 Calories (20% from Fat)
Fat 2.0g (Saturated Fat 0.4g)
Protein 0.8g Carbohydrate 18.0g
Cholesterol 0mg Sodium 111mg

INDEX